CHISELED BY THE MASTER'S HAND

CHISELED BY THE MASTER'S HAND

ERWIN LUTZER

While this book is intended for the reader's personal enjoyment and profit, it is also intended for group study.

A leader's guide with Reproducible Response Sheets is available from your local bookstore or from the publisher.

VICTOR BOOKS

A DIVISION OF SCRIPTURE PRESS PUBLICATIONS INC.
USA CANADA ENGLAND

Unless otherwise noted, Scripture quotations are from
the *New American Standard Bible*, © the Lockman
Foundation 1960, 1962, 1963, 1968, 1971, 1972,
1973, 1975, 1977; other quotations are from the
Authorized (King James) Version (KJV).

Library of Congress Cataloging-in-Publication Data

Lutzer, Erwin W.
    Chiseled by the Master's hand / by Erwin Lutzer.
      p.   cm. — (Life-in-perspective series)
    ISBN 1-56476-059-6
    1. Peter, the Apostle, Saint.
    2. Christian life — 1960-
    I. Title. II. Series.
    BS2515.L87 1993
    225.9'2 — dc20   92-47022
                                            CIP

---

1 2 3 4 5 6 7 8 9 10 Printing / Year 97 96 95 94 93

Contents

To Nick Girka
who is young in the faith,
sensitive in spirit,
and daily chiseled by the Master's hand.

Introduction

Michelangelo, it is said, was walking past a discarded piece of marble when he exclaimed, "I see an angel in there!" His genius could see the potential others had overlooked. Of course, whether an angel ever emerged from that block of marble was dependent on the sculptor's own plan and initiative.

Christ can see possibilities in us. He could see in Zaccheus the dishonest tax collector, an honest tax collector. He could see in an immoral woman a worshiper who would delight the heart of God. He could see in Paul the persecutor, Paul the proclaimer of Christianity. And He could see in Peter the man of clay, a man of rock.

In these pages we will see how Christ changed Peter from fisherman to apostle. Peter the compulsive personality had to be molded into Peter the tough but compliant personality. His fears had to give way to faith and his instability had to become a firm foundation. The sand dune had to be changed into a rock.

As we glimpse into Peter's experiences we will be rebuked, encouraged, challenged and, above all, strengthened in our own walk with Christ. As though looking into a mirror, we will no longer see Peter, but ourselves. For the Divine Sculptor who patiently molded this fisherman continues His work in our hearts. No matter how far we might have come, He will continue to chip away at our rough spots until we see Him face to face.

Thankfully, Peter's Sculptor is ours too.

Chapter One

MEETING THE MASTER

(Read John 1:35-42)

A sculptor was asked, "How do you sculpture an elephant?" to which he replied, "I just take a block of marble and chisel away everything that isn't elephant!"

When God chooses us, He shapes us so that everything standing in the way of our usefulness is cut away. His focus is not on what we *do* but on what we *are* in the hidden parts of the soul. The shaping of character is always His first priority. People, circumstances, and the unseen battles within the heart become His chisel to fashion us after His liking. *He cuts away everything that isn't like Christ.*

The process is never finished in this life. Thankfully, we do not have to be perfect before we can know God intimately and be used for His glory. History tells us that God uses imperfect people—graciously blessing many whom we would long since have cast away. He is never finished with the raw material that is in His loving hands. Our response to His chisel, however, determines the extent of our usefulness; it determines just how much good we will do that will last for eternity.

Consider Peter, the famous apostle, the man in whose honor the elaborate Basilica in Rome was built. When Peter was growing up as a lad in Bethsaida, no one would ever have guessed that he was destined for greatness. He spent his early days fishing in the Sea of Galilee, at best had a rudimentary education and would have been willing to live his life in obscurity. He probably became acquainted with the Greek language and its culture because of the foreign influence in this Jewish town. But even after three years with Christ, he was judged to be unschooled (Acts 4:13). Yet for all that, think of what Peter accomplished!

About all we know of Peter's family is that he had a brother, Andrew, and their father's name was John. These two brothers were fishing partners with two other brothers, James and John, whose father was Zebedee. Their business was so successful that they needed hired servants to help with the trade. Incredibly, all four of these young men were eventually chosen to be the disciples of Christ.

Though he was born in Bethsaida, when Peter met Christ he was married and had moved to Capernaum. His mother-in-law was healed of a fever at the beginning of Peter's friendship with Jesus (Mark 1:29-31). Twenty years later Paul mentioned that Peter often took his wife with him on his missionary travels (1 Cor. 9:5). We can only speculate about the kind of stress his decision to follow Christ must have had on his marriage.

Mention the name *Peter* and you get a variety of responses. Some remember him for his vacillating, unpredictable comments in free-flowing discussions with Christ. Others think of his remarkable insight into the person of Christ; or in contrast, there is his fearful denial in the presence of a servant girl. Then again we remember his boldness when confronted by mobs on the Day of Pentecost. Those who have been particularly blessed by his writings (1 and 2 Peter) think of him as a theologian, the man who knew God and gave explicit instructions on how Christians should conduct themselves in a hostile world. No personality in the Bible exhibits so much faith and doubt, courage and fear, love and impulsiveness. No other disciple reveals his heart so often and so honestly. He is, in the words of Clarence McCartney, "the most vivid and intense person portrayed in the Bible."

Peter provides an excellent example of how God shapes a life, beginning with the raw material and progressing to a more finished product. The Lord's training technique includes both encouragement and rebuke, public instruction and private reflection. There was both joy and sadness, success and failure. Christ interacted more often with Peter than with any of the other apostles. Conversion itself is instantaneous, but the refinement of Peter continued throughout his lifetime. *This is nothing less than the sculpturing of the soul.*

Some would have us believe that human nature can only be modified, not changed. Liars seldom become honest, adulterers seldom return to fidelity, and addicts seldom break free from their addiction. And even if these habits change, the disposition of the heart remains essentially the same.

Christ taught, and honest people will agree, that we are all fatally flawed. "For from within, out of the heart of men, proceed the evil thoughts and fornications, thefts, murders, adulteries, deeds of coveting, and wickedness, as well as deceit, sensuality, envy, slander, pride, and foolishness. All these evil things proceed from within and defile the man" (Mark 7:21-23).

Seneca cried out in despair, "O, that a hand would come down from heaven and deliver me from my besetting sin." Peter's life is a powerful witness to the good news that a hand *has* reached down from heaven to give us supernatural help. We are not confined to our own efforts in bringing about fundamental change in our character. God has visited our planet, and because of His grace we can be different.

Peter met Christ during the powerful, albeit controversial, ministry of John the Baptist, who commanded people to repent because the Messiah would soon be revealed. This radical prophet attracted enough attention to warrant a visit from representatives of the religious establishment who wondered who he really was (John 1:19-28).

John's ministry got a boost because the people were grasping for a hope that a redeemer could come and lead them into victory against Rome. The nation was under Roman occupation, and the people responded with all of the resentment that such dominance ignites. Not only were Roman legions visible in the cities and towns, but taxes had to be paid to these self-serving foreigners. The Jews comforted themselves with the belief that the Messiah was coming, and that He would crush the Roman authorities and bring about a thoroughly Jewish state. This nationalistic pride swelled the ranks of those who listened to John's message. Little wonder some of the fishermen of Galilee made the eighty-mile trek to where John was baptizing to satisfy their curiosity.

Jesus Himself paid a visit to John, who was His cousin in the flesh. When John saw Him coming toward him near the Jordan, he cried out, "Behold, the Lamb of God who takes away the sin of the world!" (John 1:29) Then John told his disciples how he had had the privilege of baptizing the Christ, and how God Himself had borne witness that "this was the Son of God."

Two of John's disciples heard his speech and were so impressed that they left John to follow Christ to His abode. "What do you seek?" Jesus asked. They responded, "Rabbi (which translated means Teacher), where are You staying?" (v. 38) Jesus was always ready to take time for seekers, so He extended the invitation, "Come, and you will see" (v. 39). They walked with Him to where He was staying and, according to Roman custom, visited with Him from 10 o'clock in the morning until sunset.

We should marvel at Christ's accessibility to ordinary folk.

He was willing to entertain those who took the time to investigate His claims; He had the time and the disposition to answer questions and show kindness. Here was a man who understood both the motives of the heart, and its potential for either great blessing or great disaster.

These two disciples, Andrew and most likely John (the brother of James the son of Zebedee, who would become known as the "beloved Apostle"), were increasingly impressed. During those hours they became absolutely convinced that Jesus was the Christ, the promised Messiah of Israel. Incredible as it seemed, this was the One they had been waiting for!

Andrew left the meeting and immediately went to find his own brother, Peter, to blurt out the news, "We have found the Messiah!" The Greek word may be translated *eureka*, a word attributed to Archimedes upon discovering a method to determine the purity of gold. These two disciples, however, had found something of much greater value—they had found a pearl of infinite worth, the Messiah, the Lord, the King!

Andrew was not a scholar, but he knew that if his brother would meet Jesus for himself, he would come to the same conclusion. So with a heart filled with warmth and affection, Andrew brought Peter to Jesus. He discovered that he scarcely needed to introduce them to one another!

Andrew stands in sharp contrast to his flamboyant, famous brother. He is not recorded as having preached any sermons; he did not make any rash promises nor did he ask any impertinent questions. But he was active behind the scenes bringing people to Christ. Certainly this one thoughtful act alone is sufficient to assure Andrew a place in history. For those servants who are faithful in bringing a mighty servant to Christ share in that mighty servant's reward.

Few people have heard of Edward Kimball, yet he is the

Sunday School teacher who led D.L. Moody to Christ. No one knows the name of an unlettered lay preacher who preached in a primitive British chapel on the text, "Look unto Me and be ye saved, all the ends of the earth." Yet through that imperfect channel, the famous Charles Haddon Spurgeon was converted.

Andrew teaches us that when we do the good that lies at our hand, we may do more for Christ than if we perform some visible service that catches the eyes of men but misses the approval of God. God always begins His special works in secret, and only later is His plan made clear to His people. It is a high privilege to be a steppingstone for others who are destined to have a personal confrontation with Christ.

Andrew brought his brother to Christ but apparently did not have the opportunity of making a formal introduction. The moment they met, Christ looked at Peter with a gaze that held the promise of hope and power: "You are Simon the son of John; you shall be called Cephas" (v. 42). The name *Cephas* is Aramaic for Peter, which means *rock*. Christ not only knew who Peter was, He also knew who Peter would eventually become.

"You are!" is the diagnosis.

"You shall be!" is the promise.

Peter, with his knowledge of the Old Testament, might well have thought of Abram, whose name was changed by God to Abraham (the father of many); and Jacob, whose name was changed to Israel (a prince with God). God never changes a man's name without also changing his character or position.

To know Simon's name was to know his present character and life. To rename him was proof that he would become a different kind of person. And only Christ, who had both the knowledge and power to shape this man according to God's intentions, could make such a prediction.

Such knowledge and power can be both frightening and comforting. If Jesus knows us completely and yet loves us enough to reshape our lives, we can take heart. And although His chisel will hurt, in the end it will be for our good. To be molded by the Master's hand is an honor indeed.

Peter learned, as we all must, that standing in Christ's presence brings both despair and hope. Those who reject Him will wish they had not been born; those who submit will become a masterpiece that will endure forever as a credit to the Divine Sculptor.

Christ Knows Who We Are

"You are Simon!"

Occasionally God selects His leaders from among those of noble birth, the intelligent, or the gifted. But usually He uses the common clay pot or stones of ordinary grain. The unadorned and simple home of this fisherman would be the quarry from which this stone would be dug. If we had done a study of Peter's humble origins, we would never have guessed that he would eventually become the stuff of saints.

Christ knew Simon's true character, his strengths and weaknesses, his aspirations, insecurities, and disappointments. Christ knew his vocation, his secret thoughts. He knew how Simon would respond to all the twists and turns that lay in his path. Christ's knowledge was so exhaustive that He could have written a whole library of books on one whose name was Simon, son of John!

Counselors tell us that their clients are often not entirely honest. All of us want to put ourselves in the best possible light. Who of us would reveal our hidden thoughts to others? Yet, without our saying a word, without a chance to put the best possible spin on our shortcomings and temptations, *Christ knows!*

Our lives and thoughts are an open book to Jesus: "There

is no creature hidden from His sight, but all things are open and laid bare to the eyes of Him with whom we have to do" (Heb. 4:13). He knows our names and a lot more besides.

He also knew Peter's lineage: "You are Simon the son of John." Some people think they were born into the wrong family. Others do not know their parents, because of either death or adoption. With the families of our nation being so torn apart, those who struggle with the uncertainty of their family roots often despair of becoming emotionally whole. Yet, *Christ knows!*

On January 5, 1527, Felix Manz was brought from the Wellenberg prison in Zurich, Switzerland, to the Limmat River, where he was drowned because of his faith in Christ. His crime was that he rejected infant baptism and was re-baptized as an adult on profession of his faith in Christ. As he was pushed into the water, the voice of his mother was heard above the waves, urging her son to remain true to the faith.

This famous martyr was an illegitimate son of a priest who practiced immorality, a sin that was almost as rampant in those days as it is today. This is proof, if proof is needed, that God can mightily use those who are conceived out of wedlock. Christ is not limited by our family history. The Christ who knew Peter's lineage knows about all of the skeletons in our family closet.

Take heart, you who are ashamed of your family history. You stand in the presence of Christ who loves you and has a plan for your life, no matter your family roots. His providential care is not limited by your lineage. He is prepared to lovingly mold anyone's offspring if they submit to His sure hand.

Christ knows not only what is true of us, but what would have been true of us if our circumstances had been different. If Peter had been born in another town and to a different family, he would have had quite a different history. Christ knows what Peter would have been like in all of these situations.

Have you been misunderstood? Have your enemies spread lies with the express intention of ruining your good name? Christ knows everything; He knows it fully, accurately, and without bias. And though He knows your weaknesses, He also loves you and knows He can change you.

When Christ died on the cross, we were on His mind. In fact, we were known by Him from eternity past. He is not about to forget about us now.

Let me repeat: *Christ knows who we are!*

Christ Knows Who We Can Become

There is a story of a painter who saw a beggar whose clothes were tattered, hair unkempt, and his face dirty. The artist decided to paint the man as he might have looked if he had had the dignity of a job and home. When he invited the beggar to see the painting, the beggar did not recognize himself. "That's me?" he asked. "Yes," said the artist, "that's what I see in you." For the first time in years the aging man was given hope. He promised, "By God's grace I'm going to be the kind of man you see me to be!"

Christ, the omnipotent artist, saw not the Peter who *was* but the Peter he *would become*. " 'You are Simon the son of John; you shall be called Cephas' (which translated means Peter)" (John 1:42). As already mentioned, the name *Cephas* is Aramaic for Peter, which means "rock." Rock is formed by sand that is under pressure and heat. Peter would have his character changed from instability to stability. *Simon* was the name given to him by his parents; *Rock* was the name given to him by Christ.

What does the name *Rock* affirm?

First, we think of *strength*. A rock signifies stability, dependability, and permanence. The man who builds his house on the rock can withstand the storms of life. Though everything else may be swept away, the rock stands firm. Simon's insecurities and fears would be turned into a monument to God's unfailing grace.

Second, a rock symbolizes *permanence.* A rock remains though all else be swept away. When a dam breaks, spilling torrents of water into the area, all the sand along the riverbanks is washed away. But the huge boulders remain. So it will be at the end of the age; everything we did that was not tied to God and His eternal purposes will be carried away by the flood of God's judgment. The rocks will remain.

When is the last time Peter is referred to in the New Testament? We might be tempted to say that it is in the Book of Acts or in his own epistles. But his name is inscribed in the New Jerusalem, and will be there forever as a testimony to his faithfulness. We read, "And the wall of the city had twelve foundation stones, and on them were the twelve names of the twelve apostles of the Lamb" (Rev. 21:14). Peter's name, along with that of the other apostles, is permanently engraved in one of the pillars of the Holy City!

Peter and his contribution to Christ's work will survive the destruction of the earth and the burning up of all of its elements. This rock will endure long after the flames of judgment have done their damage. There he is, a fisherman, but also *a pillar in the eternal city of God.*

We cannot be sure that Peter was converted during this first encounter with Christ. Yet he left that initial interview both elated and despairing. He must have wondered whether Christ really understood who he was, a rough fisherman filled with the frailty and desires of the flesh. How could he ever become known as "the man of rock"? Yet his affection had been won, his soul stirred with restless passion. Now that he had met Christ, he would never be the same. Though he had an ordinary past, he would have an extraordinary future.

Christ's words provided the hope and motivation Peter needed to think beyond the immediate pressures of earning a living. In moments of loneliness, misunderstanding, and failure, he could reflect on Christ's prediction that he would become a man of stability and strength. Regardless of the past and present, he was promised a rewarding future.

The Stonecutter had begun by hewing a rough stone from the quarry. From now on the work would progress at a reasonable pace. Looking at the untrimmed edges of this obscure piece of rock, the Master saw a saint. The chisel would do its work.

Christ Can Change Us

Why could Jesus be so confident that Peter would become a great man? He was making a promise, not just because He knew the future but because He knew that He had the power to shape the future. His promise was not based on a whim but on known resources. *Christ can guarantee the future because it is in His hands!*

Simon, I believe, was the firstborn, the leader among his siblings. In the New Testament he asked more questions than all the other disciples combined; he was the only one who tried to walk on water; the one who made the great confession regarding who Christ was; and also, the one who promised he would never deny Christ. Firstborns often have just such leadership qualities that need to be honed and directed.

A difference in temperament, often found among brothers and sisters, should be a cause for rejoicing, not unflattering comparison. The Divine Sculptor does not manufacture saints as one might make statues in a factory. He delights to take diverse raw material and make the unexpected. The varied personalities, gifts, desires, and aptitudes of all God's people remain intact but are brought under His direction. Then, like the different parts of a body, each of us contributes to the strength and coordination of the whole.

Since Christ is now shaping us just as He did Peter, we need to take a moment to learn some lessons about how the Master Sculptor does His work. Here are some basic observations.

First, we are struck with the realization that human actions and divine providence converge to accomplish the will of God. Andrew, no doubt, thought that the decision to bring Peter to Christ was his alone; this was a natural response of someone who wanted his brother to share good news. Yet years later Jesus would explain that those who came to Him were drawn by the Holy Spirit. *The visible actions of men are often the invisible actions of God.* Christ is the One who chooses the stones He desires to fashion (15:16).

Second, Christ begins the transformation by forgiving our sins and changing our disposition. John the Baptist said of Him, "Behold, the Lamb of God who takes away the sin of the world!" (1:29) Here was a man who could successfully deal with the most fundamental problem of human existence. He would begin by removing Peter's sin so that this humble fisherman might establish a direct relationship with God.

Sin was covered in the Old Testament, but it was never taken away. Day by day and year by year sacrifices had to be offered with the distinct knowledge that the offenses of tomorrow would need yet another sacrifice. And even then the sacrifices covered only the sins of Israel; *this* sacrifice would take away the sins of the world!

Third, Christ can change human nature. A Christian is not merely a sinner minus his sins, but a new creation. There is a transformation of heart that is the beginning of a whole new level of human existence. This does not mean an instant life of spiritual vigor; it means simply that the potential is there for radical transformation.

Jesus used the illustration of human birth: "Truly, truly, I say to you, unless one is born again, he cannot see the kingdom of God" (3:3). When a baby is born, it has all the parts of its anatomy intact. The toes, fingers, eyes, and ears are all there; whether or not it grows depends on the nourishment and care it will receive. When we are born again, the work is complete but it is not finished. We still have growing to do.

Peter was promised that he would become a rock. Thirty years later, he wrote that all of us are stones in the living temple which God is building: "You also, as living stones, are being built up as a spiritual house for a holy priesthood, to offer up spiritual sacrifices acceptable to God through Jesus Christ" (1 Peter 2:5). The same Lord who took up the chisel to bring about a new Peter is the One who uses His chisel to shape us too.

Only gradually would Peter understand how much he really needed to be changed. The gap between what he was and what he would become was much wider than he realized. He would learn that *he must be willing to admit who he was before Christ could change him into who he could become.*

Before we look at how Christ shaped Peter's life, let us each identify our real name, the word that best describes where we are spiritually right now. Then let us think of how Christ can rename us for His glory.

Is our name *anxiety*?	Christ can name us *peace*.
Is our name *addiction*?	Christ can name us *freedom*.
Is our name *rejection*?	Christ can name us *acceptance*.
Is our name *bitter*?	Christ can name us *love*.
Is our name *fear*?	Christ can name us *courage*.
Is our name *guilty*?	Christ can name us *forgiven*.

There is no transformation without pain. With every bit of change, we die a bit more to ourselves. The Divine Sculptor wounds us that He might mold us; He breaks us that He might straighten us.

As the shaping begins we can say with John Newton:

> I am not what I ought to be,
> I am not what I want to be,
> I am not what I hope to be.
> But thank God
> I am not what I used to be.

The first step is to submit to the Man with a loving heart who has a chisel in His hand. "You *are* . . . but you shall *be*. . . ."

Chapter Two

SURPRISED BY A MIRACLE

(Read Luke 5:1-11)

The Divine Sculptor does not work with marble, but with human beings who are actively involved in the shaping process. God begins His serious work by showing us just how much needs to be done. To be effective, the chisel must open the soul to self-awareness. As emphasized in the last chapter, we must know who we *are* before we can expect to be changed into who we can *become*.

Christ knew that sculpturing is an individual process; each person must feel the blows and respond to the grinding wheel. The men Christ selected would be His representatives to carry on His work. Like the rabbis of old, He knew that His greatest ministry would not be with the crowds but with individuals ignited with His fire. These men would follow Him, learning His doctrine and His practices. They would carry the torch to their generation and eventually to the world.

Creative teacher that He was, Christ used the common experiences of the disciples to teach some uncommon lessons. Several of His chosen followers were fishermen by trade, a vocation that prepared them for their new calling. After these men had met Christ along the banks of the Jordan, they went back to their homes expecting to continue in their fishing business. Their search for the Messiah had ended, but the need for their daily bread continued.

What a change one day can bring! A few months before they had gone to meet the Messiah, but now *He came to meet them.* As He walked along the shore of Galilee, Jesus saw the brothers Andrew and Peter casting a net into the sea. He called to them, "Follow Me, and I will make you to become fishers of men" (Mark 1:17).

What a novel idea! They had never observed anyone "catching men," so they were puzzled by His words. But the Master would soon teach them a lesson that would clarify what fishing for men was all about. And if Peter and his companions learned this lesson well, their lives would be changed forever.

In Luke 5:1-11 we have an account of a miracle that assured the disciples that fishing for men would be successful. One morning as the villages around Galilee were awakening to the life of a new day, a crowd surrounded Christ as He strolled along the shore. The size of the multitude increased and He found Himself pushed close to the water's edge. Providentially, Peter and his companions had just come to shore and were putting their nets away, but their boats were empty. So Jesus climbed into Peter's boat and asked him to push out a short distance; then He sat down in the boat and began to teach. This arrangement enabled Him to speak to more people and be more clearly seen at the same time.

Wondrous condescension! Jesus could have found some other way to speak to the crowd so that He would not have had to depend on Peter's kindness. But, though He has infinite resources, *He lets us help Him!* When He had finished His lesson, Jesus turned to Peter and said, "Put out into the deep water and let down your nets for a catch" (v. 4). But the command seemed foolish. There were some well-known reasons why this was the wrong time and place to fish.

Here we have a firsthand example of Christ's chiseling process. Though His target was all four of these would-be disciples, the sharpest pain would come to Peter's soul.

Peter Is Wondering

Standing in a boat hardly qualified one to be known as an expert fisherman! Peter and his companions had had a difficult night, for though they cast their net many times, they caught nothing. Without a word they finished cleaning their nets and were putting them away for the day. That's why they felt so surprised when they heard Christ say, "Put out into the deep water and let down your nets for a catch."

There were some rather well-known rules about fishing in Galilee. For years Peter and his friends had observed the habits of fish, the hours and places most likely to yield a catch. If his peers would have given him advice, he would have resented it. But now Peter was confronted with the command of a Man whom he had recently come to respect; a Man he was convinced was the promised Messiah. How should he respond to this request, though it seemed so obviously wrong?

Peter was exhausted from the failure of the past night and wanted to make the point that they had already tried their best: "Master, we worked hard all night and caught nothing, but at Your bidding I will let down the nets" (v. 5). We can almost hear a sigh of hopelessness in his voice. If they didn't catch fish at the best time, how could he expect to catch any now? But whether the command was wise or not, to his everlasting credit *Peter obeyed.*

There were two reasons why Christ's command would have appeared foolish. First, this was the *wrong time.* In Galilee the best time to fish was during the night and the early morning. This explains why they had been out all night. Even though they had caught nothing, there always was a much better chance of catching fish during the night than during the day. On this particular night, the fish were not hungry and were not attracted to the movement of the nets in the water. If none were caught at night, there would certainly be none in the heat of the morning.

Second, this was the *wrong place*. Every fisherman knew that the best place to catch fish was along the shore, not in the deep water. To put out into the deep with a boat laden with nets would bring ridicule from those who lingered along the shore. Only a carpenter would not know these time-honored rules of fishing!

Foolish or not, Peter could not escape this clear command. If Christ was to be his master, His authority would extend to Peter's fishing business. There cannot be two captains on the same boat. Dutifully, he let down the nets for a catch.

To his surprise, we read, "And when they had done this, they enclosed a great quantity of fish; and their nets began to break; and they signaled to their partners in the other boat, for them to come and help them. And they came and filled both of the boats, so that they began to sink" (vv. 6-7).

Peter left with one boat but returned with two—both filled with fish! Along with Christ's command to fish had come a miracle! Though it was the worst time and the worst place, the nets were filled with a catch.

The lesson was becoming clear: *If Peter could be successful at catching fish at Christ's command, maybe he could be successful at catching men.*

What are the two most common excuses for not witnessing about Christ? The *time* just never seems right. And the *place* seems inappropriate. Or perhaps we think that if we had the right education, or the right book, or the right technique, we would be qualified to share the Good News of the Gospel. Important though all these may be, Christ reminds us that *dependent obedience makes the difference.*

All fishermen have times when they catch nothing. Some friends of mine even drive from Chicago to Ontario to go fishing in a northern lake. Sometimes they come home with a barrel of fish, sometimes they catch few. Regardless, they still make the trip as often as they can. A real fisherman, they say, keeps fishing even when he has a string of bad days.

So it is with fishing for men. Sometimes we are successful, sometimes we aren't, but our disappointments should not discourage us. We are partners in Christ's fishing business. Paul wrote that we are "God's fellow-workers" (1 Cor. 3:9). We are never in the wrong season, nor in the wrong circumstances, when we are obedient to Christ. Waters that yield no results when we are in charge can bring a full net when we are obedient to the Lord, the God of the universe. A.T. Robertson says, "Simon was at once challenged by Jesus to fish again in the very waters where he had fished all night and caught nothing" (*Epochs in the Life of Peter* [Grand Rapids: Baker, 1976], p. 23). We often need to fish again where we have failed before, and we must get down deeper than we were before. Sometimes we must fish the same waters, reaffirming that our ship is under the complete control of our new captain.

I do not mean to imply that we should witness ("fish for men") indiscriminately. There is a time to be silent and a time to speak; there are circumstances where Christ is best served by our lives rather than our tongues. But many believers multiply excuses for not sharing their faith when the real reason is a lack of faith, a deep-seated skepticism about Christ's ability to save sinners. All of us must be reminded that when we cast our net, Christ is able to fill it.

This miracle was to be a learning experience. The Divine Sculptor was shaping the lives of Peter and his companions. If Simon had to become a rock, his obedience would have to be tested and the chisel put to his soul.

Peter Is Learning

Christ expected the disciples to make the connection between His invitation to come with Him to "catch men," and His ability to help them catch fish. When we fish for ourselves, we get the mixed results that are in keeping with our own efforts. When we fish at Christ's words, He, the Lord, is fully responsible for what we find in our nets.

Why can we fish for men and women with confidence?

First, because of Christ's *power*. Where did these fish come from? They swam into the nets at the direction of the Lord. They were compelled by a supernatural impulse to swim into waters they had naturally avoided. Whether this was the right time and place made little difference. God had spoken; *the fish of the sea were commanded and they came.*

We can be quite sure that the previous night the fish had *avoided* the nets under Christ's direction! He wanted the disciples to fail at fishing, to make the point that as the Son of God He was qualified to direct the course of men and beasts. God said that man was to "rule over the fish of the sea and over the birds of the sky and over the cattle and over all the earth, and over every creeping thing that creeps on the earth" (Gen. 1:26). Adam's authority to control the animals was lost after the Fall, but Christ, the second Adam, exercised that authority by directing the fish in Galilee to bypass the net during the night and, contrary to nature, swim into the nets in the deep water during the day.

Someone might argue that this analogy cannot apply to winning men and women to Christ because, after all, humans have free will. The argument is that people cannot be commanded by Christ to be saved since the decision is theirs, not God's. But the same Christ at whose bidding the fish came into the net often claimed that He had authority over people as well. He said when praying to the Father, "Even as Thou gavest Him [Christ] authority over all mankind, that to all whom Thou hast given Him, He may give eternal life" (John 17:2). Three times in one discourse Christ said that no man could come to Him unless drawn by His Father (6:37, 44, 65). No fish comes into the celestial net unless the Father wills it.

We should not deduce from this that human beings are animals or pawns who have no responsibility for their own decisions. But we can be certain that no one can ever choose to come to Christ unless compelled by God through the inner prompting of the Holy Spirit. Only God can overcome the natural resistance we all have to come to Christ, admitting our sinfulness and clinging to His grace.

Be our net ever so large, be our casting of it ever so skillful, be our intentions ever so worthy, *no fish will come to it unless drawn by God.* Without a divine miracle we could fish for lost souls all of our lives and catch nothing. Indeed without such a miracle, we ourselves would never have been "caught."

We should never be discouraged when casting our net. Although statistics indicate that most Christians were converted before the age of twenty-one, we have no right to predict those whom God will or will not save. God has often chosen to save hardened sinners; yes, sometimes He has saved old, rebellious sinners; sometimes old, confused, hardened sinners. "He is able to save to the uttermost those who come to God through Him, since He ever liveth to make intercession for them" (Heb. 7:25, KJV).

We can cast our nets with confidence because of Christ's power. He is the one to whom all authority in heaven and on earth is given. We are quite literally in the fishing business with God!

Second, we can fish with confidence because we are thereby *obeying Christ's command.* Despite his doubts Peter said, "But at Your bidding I will let down the nets." We don't know whether he actually thought he would catch some fish. Possibly he obeyed Christs's bare word expecting to pull the nets through the water only to have them come up empty once more. Even if Peter had not caught a single fish, we would have to commend him for doing whatever the Master commanded. Yet because of that obedience, he caught so many fish that others also were blessed by the miracle. Now that Peter was a partner with Christ, others became partners with *him*. He signaled for a second boat because the nets were beginning to break!

God does not need us to do His work on earth. He could have commanded the fish to jump into Peter's boat without using a net. Or they could have swum to shore to be caught by the hungry multitudes walking at the water's edge. He could speak and sinners would repent; He could save His elect just as Saul was converted on the way to Damascus. We could be nothing more than spectators while God does His work on earth.

But God has graciously ordained that we be co-laborers with Him as long as we live on this planet. We have the privilege of casting the nets, of bringing the fish to shore. He makes us partners in His fishing business because He wants to teach us more of Himself. Incredibly, He has chosen us to do His business!

Let's not shirk our duty to fish for men because we don't feel spiritual enough, or because we don't know enough, important though that may be. Yes, we must walk more closely with God, we must study and learn how to share our faith. But all of our excuses vanish in the presence of the Sovereign Christ. *If God has commanded us to witness, are not the results in His capable hands?*

And what if we cast our net and catch no fish? We do what every fisherman does: We fish again, perhaps even in the same waters. Our success or failure is not dependent on the number of fish we catch but on our obedience to Christ's command.

Fishing for men does not mean that we must witness to everyone we meet, or impose the Good News on those who are indifferent to their own spiritual welfare. I have learned that when we are spiritually alert, God often prepares the hearts of people and actually creates the spiritual hunger that precedes "the catch." He makes these fish swim in the direction of the net. Often we must simply pray and wait until the Heavenly Fisherman brings them in our direction.

Successful fishermen know how to use bait wisely. They know their equipment and study the habits of the fish. But they also know that they can only cast the net; the Lord alone can fill those nets according to His will.

Peter Is Worshiping

We expect Peter to be thrilled with the sight of a boatload of fish. Here is more money than he and his partners could have hoped to make in a week. Peter, we might think, is already contemplating how these extra shekels might be spent. Every fisherman gloats on a lucky day. Nothing can change our mood as rapidly as news of a financial windfall. The unexpected check in the mail, the phone call that tells us we are getting a pay raise—such experiences can quickly bring sunshine to a cloudy heart.

If Peter had embraced our modern "health and wealth" gospel, he would have approached Christ and invited Him to join his fishing business! Think of the boon it would have been to have Christ become the leading partner of the firm. Why not? After all, followers of Christ should prosper in their business!

Not so Peter. He reacted not to the startling success of that day's catch but to the Person who produced this miracle. "But when Simon Peter saw that, he fell down at Jesus' feet, saying, 'Depart from me, for I am a sinful man, O Lord!' For amazement had seized him and all his companions because of the catch of fish which they had taken. . . . And Jesus said to Simon, 'Do not fear, from now on you will be catching men' " (Luke 5:8-10).

Peter was a broken man. He clung to his Master yet also urged Him to depart—the natural response of one who both loved Christ and hated his own sinfulness. His mind was simultaneously filled with confession and adoration. *The contrast between a holy God and his own unholy self caused him to shrink back in despair.*

We may look in many places to find a clue to Peter's eventual greatness, but for now we need look no further. Profoundly aware of his own sinfulness, and equally aware of Christ's holy presence, Peter illustrates the first lesson we need to learn in service to Christ: *The depth of our worship is dependent on an awareness of the depth of our own sinfulness.*

This was the Divine Sculptor at work. The Lord had taken His chisel and opened Peter's heart. He was wounded that he might be healed; he was broken that he might be molded according to the Master's design. Peter could not see others until he saw himself; and he could not see himself until he saw the Lord.

Before Peter could work for God, God had to work in him. If he was to kindle a flame in others, he himself would first have to be lit with the divine fire. Like Isaiah, Peter had to say, "Woe is me," before he could say, "Here am I, send me." Like Moses in the presence of the burning bush, Peter had to *worship* before he could *work.*

John Bunyan says of his own experience with God, "I was more loathsome in mine own eyes than was a toad. . . . I thought none but the devil himself could equal me for inward wickedness and pollution of mind. I was both a burden and a terror to myself. How gladly would I have been anything but myself" (*Peter,* F.B. Meyer [New York: Fleming H. Revell, 1920], p. 25).

Without a knowledge of our own heart, we cannot unlock the hearts of others. When we spend the night in a hotel we have only the key to one room, but the manager has a master key that enables him to unlock every room in the building. For ministers of Christ such a key is the knowledge of one's own self. Only such awareness enables us to open the hearts of others and introduce them to the Savior who met the deepest needs of our own heart. F.B. Meyer says that those who have seen their own sinfulness "are familiar with the holes where the fish lie and the best methods of reaching them. They have infinite patience, as the Lord had patience with them. They bear gently with the erring, and with those who resent their approach, because they themselves have been compassed with infirmity" (*Peter,* p. 26).

When Peter pushed his boat into the sea that morning, he called Christ *Master.* When he returned with two boatloads of fish, he called Him *Lord* (Greek, *Kyrios,* meaning Lord or God). Like Job and Isaiah before him, Peter was in the presence of the Almighty, where he felt both despair and hope. Blessed are those who believe that repentance is a precious gift of God.

When Martin Scorsese made his blasphemous movie, *The Last Temptation of Christ,* he wrote, "What I've tried to create is a Jesus who, in a sense, is just like any other guy in the street. In his struggles to reach God and find God, he reflects all of our struggles. I thought it would give us all hope."

What delusion! Far from giving us hope, a Jesus who is just like us would leave us in our hopelessness. Peter's pitiful state of despair was the sign of true hope. We do not need a Christ who is like us; we need a Christ who is Lord, King. We need a Christ who can command fish to come into a net. A Christ so sinless, so perfect, and so divine that He can bring us to God. In His presence we are filled with a sense of our own inexcusable sinfulness, and also with adoring wonder.

Luther said that we cannot reach heaven until we first descend to hell. We cannot be God's children until we see ourselves as children of the devil. For in such a self-revelation, says Luther, we finally see God. The sheer power of Christ's holy presence sent a shaft of light into Peter's soul. He had met the Holy Son of God. *The chisel had hit its mark.*

As we toured the famous Rijksmuseum in Amsterdam, our tour guide told us that about 10 percent of Rembrandt's paintings were paintings of himself. But far from being an exercise in self-aggrandizement, Rembrandt was a humble Christian who painted himself just as he was, with no embellishments. Artists have often wondered why he did not take advantage of his gifted hand and paint himself with just a touch of flattery, since his physical form was far from handsome. But Rembrandt remarked, "Unless I can paint myself just as I am, I cannot paint others as they are."

Until we see ourselves for what we are in the presence of God, we will never be able to see others for what they are. There on his knees, filled with revulsion for his own sin and with a desire for holiness, Peter learned the first lesson in becoming a "fisher of men." Spiritual growth always involves a progressive knowledge of our own sinfulness. Someone has said that *in heaven the biggest crown will not go to the biggest head.* The hidden parts of the soul that we once thought were safe, harmless, or innocent become evil when exposed to the divine light.

Now that Peter had faced his sinfulness, Christ took his fear away. How relieved he was when he heard the voice of his beloved Master, "Do not fear, from now on you will be catching men" (v. 10). A.T. Robertson says that this expression means, "You will catch men alive." Though men are more difficult to catch alive in spiritual nets than fish are in ordinary nets, Peter would be working for a Man who is able to bring men to God. This was the assurance he needed that he could be successful in serving Christ though his heart was defiled by sin. Of course Christ would not abandon Peter, for His people are the objects of His affection.

On the Day of Pentecost Peter let down his net and it encompassed 3,000 men and women. In the house of Cornelius, his net had scarcely touched the "water" when it began to fill. If in Peter's first encounter with Christ he was given a promise of what he would become (a *rock*), here he is given a promise of what he will do *(fish for men)*. We may not be sure that he was converted on the banks of the Jordan, but here for certain he was a changed man.

Now that he had understood who Christ was, Peter was commanded to follow Him: "And when they had brought their boats to land, they left everything and followed Him" (v. 11). By asking His disciples to follow Him, Christ did not diminish the work of fishing. He Himself grew up in the home of a carpenter, lending His dignity to manual labor. But Peter and his three other companions were called to the specialized ministry of apostleship, and this was a full-time job. Christ would have to provide for their daily bread.

If we should ask, "How do I become a fisher of men?" the answer is unchanged—"Follow Me." The nearer we are to Jesus, the easier it will be to cast our net and find it filled with hungry men and women. Peter was brought to Christ by Andrew; eventually he would in turn bring thousands to Christ. The thrill of catching fish along the shores of Galilee would soon be replaced by the exuberance of catching the more important fish that would populate the celestial sea.

Christ did not link up with Peter's fishing business. *Peter linked up with Christ's fishing business.* The man who commanded the fish to come into Peter's net would now command men and women to come to God. And Peter, who knew how to fish, would have the privilege of enlisting others to help him bring the full nets to shore.

That day Peter met the True Fisherman. Now he would catch men, just as he himself had been caught by a Man from Galilee.

Chapter Three

WHILE WALKING ON WATER, HE SANK

(Read Matthew 14:22-36)

While we were visiting Leipzig, Germany, our tour guide pointed to a monument of Goethe, the author of "Faust." The head of the statue is turned toward the university but his feet are pointed in the direction of the Auerbach beer hall! What a graphic picture of competing loyalties!

Each of us struggles with conflicting loyalties; we love Christ but are distracted by the lure of our sinful nature within and the pressure of circumstances without. These compelling voices vie for our allegiance. We sometimes feel as if our faith in God is simply not powerful enough to weather the storms. A friend of mine with a rare disease was faithful to Christ for many years but eventually chose to plunge headlong into the rebellion of the world. Before his untimely death from alcohol he said, "God just gave me more temptation than I could bear."

How can we be successful in our walk with Christ? How can we follow Him without being distracted by the world, the flesh, and the devil? How can we follow Him with our heart as well as our head and our feet? How do we manage the fears that would engulf us?

In Matthew 14:22-36 Christ taught Peter how to survive a storm. If he was to be a faithful man despite impending powerful opposition, Peter would have to learn the secret of standing against contrary winds. Again the Master Teacher chose to use a common experience to teach an uncommon lesson. A storm on Galilee would become a prototype of the storms of life.

Christ had just fed 5,000 men (the total crowd may have been 10,000 to 15,000) with five loaves and two fish. As might be expected, the multitude was impressed. Wouldn't it be wonderful to crown such a man king? Moses had fed the Israelites with bread; it only made sense that Messiah would outdo Moses in providing for the hungry people.

The crowd followed Christ, hoping He would not get away. They would nominate Him king by acclamation, whether He wanted the position or not. Surely with enough accolades coming in His direction, He could be persuaded to take such an honor.

As happened so often, Christ disappointed them by escaping from their presence. In John we read, "Jesus therefore perceiving that they were intending to come and take Him by force, to make Him king, withdrew again to the mountain by Himself alone" (John 6:15).

Jesus was not seduced by their praise. He calmly compelled His disciples to get into a boat and go ahead of Him to the other side of the lake while He sent the multitudes away. He aborted the plans of the king-makers and escaped to the hills of Galilee to pray. There He spent perhaps seven or eight hours by Himself in the presence of His Heavenly Father.

As the pole of a compass points north when unobstructed, so the heart of our Lord was constantly seeking the delight of the Father's fellowship. He seized every opportunity to commune with the One who had sent Him. There on the hilltop the will of the Father was again clarified and the submission of the Son reaffirmed. He knew that for now He was sent to the world to be a Savior and not a King.

Even as He prayed, Jesus knew that His disciples had to learn to trust His presence though He was physically absent from them. As a mother bird thrusts her young ones from the nest that they might find their own wings, so Christ wanted the disciples to be on their own in the coming storm. Though they were beyond the range of His physical sight, those men were still the focus of His care and attention.

Usually the disciples could row across the sea in an hour or two, but this night they were battling the worst storm they could remember. Powerful winds from Mount Hermon lashed the water into a fury, and the disciples were terrified. We read, "But the boat was already many stadia away from the land, battered by the waves; for the wind was contrary. And in the fourth watch of the night He came to them, walking upon the sea. And when the disciples saw Him walking on the sea, they were frightened, saying, 'It is a ghost!' And they cried out for fear" (Matt. 14:24-26). After seven or eight hours they had only gone three or four miles (John 6:19). Then, in the middle of their distress, Christ came to them.

Notice these preliminary observations. First, *although the disciples could not see Jesus when He was praying on the hilltop, He could see them.* He knew the longitude and latitude of their boat and was watching every minute. Perhaps you've learned, as we all must, that the storms of life may hide the face of God; yet He is watching us, monitoring our movements. And when push comes to shove in life—as it so often does—*it is more important that God see us than that we see Him.* Rest assured, He is watching you as you battle your own personal storm.

Second, let us remember that *the disciples were in this squall through obedience to Christ.* Sometimes we have the mistaken notion that a storm is proof that we are "out of the will of God." Yet, it is in the center of God's will—it is in obedience to Him—that we sometimes encounter the most fierce opposition. Let's not fall into the error of thinking that we have made a wrong decision just because we are sailing into a storm. Sometimes our greatest trials come because we are walking in obedience to Christ's command.

Third, notice that *the cause of their fear eventually became a source of their comfort and joy.* They didn't recognize Christ, but He was on His way to help them. This terrifying ghost, this phantom, was a hidden blessing. The bad news you or I received recently may well have been Christ simply trying to put His arms around us!

Fourth, *Christ came at the right time*—the fourth watch of the night was approximately 4 in the morning. They had been out on the sea since the prior evening but simply hadn't made any progress. They assumed that this time Christ had given them a command they could not keep. Try as they might, they simply weren't able to obey His instructions to "go to the other side." But at their moment of desperation, Christ appeared to help them. Christ knew how much they could take, and met them at their darkest hour.

Christ can calm storms, but He can also guide His people through them. As was so often the case, He taught Peter a lesson to the benefit of the rest of the disciples. Here are three snapshots of Peter that show the sequence of his learning experience. Step by step he is molded by the Divine Sculptor, for his benefit but also for ours.

Peter Saw Christ

"But immediately Jesus spoke to them, saying, 'Take courage, it is I; do not be afraid' " (v. 27). Peter instantly recognized that voice! This was not a ghost or phantom, but His Lord, the omnipotent One! His Master had found them on this tempestuous lake because He knew the intimate details of their hopeless fight against nature.

We've all been misunderstood; perhaps no one has taken the time to find out our side of the story. We can't tell our private struggles to those who are quick to judge, those who have never felt the power of our temptations, those who have never burned with the frustrations of our unmet desires. Yet there is One who knows, who understands, and who loves His people. The all-knowing Lord sees us as our boat is battered by the storms of life. A friend who knows us but is powerless to help *is* of some comfort. Christ, however, has not only knowledge but power—the ability to actually intervene in the crucial moments when we are about to give up.

According to the laws of nature, Jesus should not have been able to walk on water. There is a law of physics that says, "The buoyant force exerted by a liquid is equal to the weight of the water displaced." That means simply that water will carry an object only to the extent of the weight of the water which has been displaced by that object. Jesus should have sunk to His shoulders, eventually becoming just as helpless in the storm as the disciples. But He is God, Lord over the forces of nature and over the law of gravity. *He walked on the raging waters of Galilee with the confidence of One who was treading on a marble floor.*

According to John, Christ walked for about four miles (John 6:19). This was the Christ who had commanded the fish and they swam into the net; this was the Christ who had turned water into wine. And now the waves and the winds were under His command. The Christ whom Peter saw was the Triumphant One, the One whose power was displayed in creating the universe.

When facing temptation, the disappointments of ill health, or the crumbling of our well-laid plans, *our first and greatest need is always to have a new vision of Christ.* At such a moment there is hope even in despair. Christ must become as real to us as the storm itself.

Peter Saw an Opportunity

If we had been in the boat, we would have been content to know that Christ was finally coming to help us. But Peter saw this as a wonderful opportunity. "And Peter answered Him and said, 'Lord, if it is You, command me to come to You on the water.' And He said, 'Come!' And Peter got out of the boat and walked on the water and came toward Jesus" (Matt. 14:28-29).

Although Peter was impetuous, often responding to life by impulse rather than careful thought, we must give him credit for seizing this opportunity. He didn't jump into the water presumptuously, saying, "Lord, here I come, save me!" No, he requested Christ's permission: "If it is You, command me to come to You on the water." Clearly, Christ was pleased with the request and responded with a simple word, "Come."

This was not a stunt orchestrated so that Peter could parade his heroism in the presence of his peers. Peter made this request because he loved Christ and couldn't wait to be near Him. He was too impatient to wait for Christ to come to the boat; he had to meet the Master *en route.*

For a brief moment Peter was actually walking on the water with Christ! If we had had a video camera, we would have seen two people defying the law of gravity, two individuals participating in a miracle. As far as we know, throughout all of history only two people have ever walked on water—Christ and Peter. (As the saying goes, all others who claim they have, only know where the rocks are!) If Peter had kept cool, gazing at Jesus, he could have walked all the way to his Master. *Christ took the waves and made them as a rock beneath Peter's feet.*

Why do all of us so often find ourselves in storms? Why are the trials of life so persistent, so unrelenting? Thirty years later, Peter himself would write, "In this you greatly rejoice, even though now for a little while, if necessary, you have been distressed by various trials, that the proof of your faith, being more precious than gold which is perishable, even though tested by fire, may be found to result in praise and glory and honor at the revelation of Jesus Christ" (1 Peter 1:6-7).

Our faith is precious to God. And only in a trial can faith come to its fullest expression. Storms keep our eyes riveted on Jesus.

Peter Saw the Wind

"But seeing the wind, he became afraid, and beginning to sink, he cried out, saying, 'Lord, save me!' " (Matt. 14:30) What caused Peter to be distracted? Why did he shift his eyes from Christ? He had a moment of self-awareness, the sensation that he was doing something which under normal conditions was impossible. He knew that the wind and the waves were more powerful than he; he knew that he did not have the power to tame the unpredictable powers of nature; and yet for this brief moment there he was, walking on water with his Master.

But the pressure of the wind and the noise of the waves distracted him; he turned to face them and immediately began to sink. In a flash he realized he was just as helpless as he thought himself to be. *He failed because he looked away from Jesus.*

There is a place for long prayers; indeed we should spend much time praying privately and publicly. But this was one of those times when only a short prayer was possible. In desperation Peter cried out, "Lord, save me!" And those three simple words captured the attention and intervention of Christ. The Master graciously stretched out His hand and lifted Peter out of the water. "O you of little faith, why did you doubt?" (v. 31)

Peter has often been criticized for his lack of faith. But we must commend him for taking the risk of walking on the water. He could have stayed in the relative safety of the boat with the other disciples. Some people have never failed simply because they have never attempted anything of significance. Those who have never stepped out of a boat should not be critical of those who do. Leslie B. Flynn says that a believing Peter who is wet is better than a doubting Thomas who is dry!

Of course, to Peter's credit, he attempted the impossible only because he heard Christ's command, "Come." Without such explicit instruction, jumping out of the boat would have been folly and suicide. Also, he took the risk alone. If indeed this was a phantom and not the Lord, only he would suffer the consequences.

Peter's Lessons

What lessons must we learn in order to navigate the storms of life? First, *we must give careful attention to the promises of Scripture.* If the disciples had clung to Christ's every word, they could have enjoyed their battle against the waves, absolutely assured that no harm would come to them. Why? Because when Christ said good-bye to them that evening, He expressly said that they were to "go to the other side" (v. 22).

If the Master of the Universe said they were to arrive on Galilee's eastern shore, they should have known that, come what may, they would make it! Some of those disciples were chosen to die a martyr's death, so there was not a chance that they would drown now in Galilee. Christ asked Peter, "O you of little faith, why did you doubt?" If only they had listened and believed, fear would have vanished.

Christ's promise to the disciples the night before, as well as His command to Peter, was unconditional. It was not, "Come if the wind will allow it," or, "Come if the water is not too deep," or, "Come if you have the strength to fight the storm." No, that single word "Come" was more powerful to Peter than all the opposition and weariness that permeated his bones. Neither angels nor demons nor men can withhold God's blessings if we respond to His invitation. Though there was much greater danger to Peter attempting to walk on the water than there would have been had he stayed on the boat, he was perfectly safe as long as he depended on the power of Christ's single word, "Come."

Christ's instructions to His disciples that they "go to the other side" was also a specific promise to them and has to be understood in that context. Christ did not always promise them such deliverance; but He did often talk to them about heaven, their eventual destination (John 14:1-3). Christ is with His people in every storm, even if the storm should kill them. Regardless of what happens on earth, our place in heaven is assured. No storm on earth can disturb the calm of heaven.

I must caution, however, that it is necessary to interpret the promises of God correctly. Some have been disappointed because they have believed God for miracles that He has not specifically promised. For example, He has not promised that the sick will always be healed or that His people will be spared accidents, illness, or even violence. His promises state that He is with us through the trials of life, but not that we will be exempt from the tragedies that befall other mortals. *Sometimes He calms the storms on the lake; sometimes He calms the storm in our heart.*

To believe our Lord's explicit promises is our first assignment.

A second lesson: *The water that threatens to be over our head is under Christ's feet!* All of us encounter winds of adversity, storms that cause us to lose our financial balance, or a health breakdown that threatens our emotional and physical well-being. Or maybe it's a relationship gone sour that has caused us emotional distress. That situation, no matter how painful, is one that Christ has fully under His control. Today He sits with it under His feet. Let us see Christ walking over the sea of God's wrath and inviting us to join Him. Let us see Christ triumphing over the sting of death and inviting us to join Him. *Let us see Him at the right hand of God the Father, with us at His side!*

Just this morning I spoke to a woman on the telephone telling me about her excruciating divorce. Her husband had been unfaithful, and now wants joint custody of the children. There is little reason to think that he actually loves his children. (If he did he should have continued to live with their mother!) He wants to assuage his guilt, to prove that he is a good dad who loves his kids after all. Fighting for the children is his way of venting his hostility toward his wife. The children are a bargaining chip in this selfish game of hateful revenge.

With the story of Peter fresh in my mind I told her, "Regardless of how intently you look at Christ, you must realize that the storm will not stop. The wind will continue to howl and the waves will continue to rise, but you must keep looking and walking." Christ is totally aware of her plight. There will be tears and pain ahead, but by focusing on the triumphant Christ, she can make it. Yes, the waters that threaten to drown her are the waters upon which Christ is walking.

There is a final lesson: *The power of our feet is dependent on the focus of our eyes.* Goethe looked to the university but walked to the beer cellar, proving that his education did not have the strength to change him. Knowledge alone will not break destructive habits; we need a miracle on the inside. When we gaze on Christ, we are granted the power to do the supernatural—to take charge of our situation and to survive the storm.

What was Peter's greatest enemy? Not the storm, nor the waves, but *doubt was his greatest adversary!* There was no need to calculate the speed of the wind, there was no need to measure the depth of the water, for none of these forces could keep Peter from his victory. Doubt and doubt alone was the only enemy that could make Peter fall.

Even if the wind is calm, we will still drown if we fail to look at Christ. Hugh Martin writes, "You will sink through the *waters* whether the *wind* be boisterous or blow softly from the south. In either case it matters not. But if you stand firm on the waters in Christ's name, sharing His dominion over sin and the curse, and Satan, and the world, and death — oh! Then no danger can arise from the wind: it must be all from unbelief" (*Simon Peter*, [Carlisle, Pa.: The Banner of Truth Trust, 1967], pp. 51–52).

A high-wire performer said that he must walk the wire concentrating completely on a fixed point on the other side. If he has his attention diverted by looking at someone beneath him or if he were to glance at the audience, he could lose his balance. Concentration is the key to walking where others have fallen.

How long did it take for Peter to sink when he looked at the wind? Perhaps only a second or two and he was on his way down. In the countless times I have failed Christ, I have learned that even a few minutes of broken fellowship can cause me to drown in the storm that seeks to destroy me. The strength of Satan or the intensity of our trials is not what forces us to fall; *unbelief is always our mortal enemy.*

A moment of uncontrolled anger can cause us to say words that destroy a relationship. If self-pity is nurtured, it can lead to hopeless depression and despair. How long does it take for us to be overcome by fear once we focus on those fears rather than on Christ? Once we have opened the door to lust, it can invade our hearts in a matter of seconds. All of these temptations and others like them can engulf us in a moment of time. And the more we are pulled in these directions, the greater their control of us becomes. If we do not diligently focus our eyes on Christ, we will lose our balance even in the small storms of life. "The steadfast of mind Thou wilt keep in perfect peace, because he trusts in Thee" (Isa. 26:3).

While flying from Chicago to Cleveland, I sat next to a retired airplane pilot. He said that many people have the mistaken notion that commercial jet planes are safer than light planes that carry only a few passengers. As proof of this perception, people cite statistics which tell us that light planes crash more often than the bigger commercial jets.

He insisted that the smaller planes are built just as safely as the bigger ones, but they have more crashes because of inexperienced pilots. These pilots often make a fundamental mistake in flying a small plane: They disbelieve their instrument panel. Their inner sense of direction tells them that the plane is gaining altitude and they steer the aircraft according to this intuition. Or perhaps they feel the plane is turning and they make adjustments based on their own innate sense of direction. And because they take these inner signals seriously, they eventually crash. In summary, he said, "Inexperienced pilots take too much information from their own sense experience."

Perhaps you feel as if you are ready to crash. You have looked at the waves, you have felt the force of gale winds, and you think you can't make it through another day. Just as a pilot must blindly trust his instruments and not his intuition, so we must focus our eyes on Christ and not the storm. When we look to Him, He will help us do the supernatural, He will help us walk through life's most turbulent times.

And how do we focus on Christ? Unfortunately, we often look for new spiritual secrets and neglect that which is most basic. First of all, we keep our focus through the Word of God—read it by the chapter, and memorize it by the verse.

Though we've heard it before, we must be reminded to absorb the Scriptures internally. This will help us meditate and focus on Christ and His power alone.

Second, there is prayer, those intimate moments when we share our cherished dreams and hopes with the Risen Christ. This intercession must be developed and strengthened. In His presence we can be honest, sharing our hurts or anger. Like David, we will find our soul refreshed.

Then third, our songs/hymns can be used to lift our hearts to God. When the words are in our minds, they stay with us for the rest of the day.

Finally, we must remember that there is strength within the body of Christ. Through the friendship and love of others we are encouraged to carry on.

Today, Christ walks over your troubled waters. He stands triumphantly defying all the laws of nature and human dynamics. He invites us to look to Him, to share His victory and His triumph. He wants the focus of our eyes and the direction of our feet pointed toward the same destination.

> Turn your eyes upon Jesus,
> Look full in His wonderful face,
> And the things of earth will grow strangely dim
> In the light of His glory and grace.

Like Peter we must learn that a steady eye on Christ will take us through many a powerful storm.

Chapter Four

NOWHERE ELSE TO GO

(Read John 6:60-71)

There is a story about a monastery in Portugal perched high on a 300-foot cliff. It can be reached only by a terrifying ride in a swaying basket. The basket is pulled with a single rope by several strong men who labor as they pull their cargo up the sheer cliff. One American tourist became nervous as he began the journey because he noticed that the rope was old and frayed. "How often do you change the rope?" he shouted to the monk as the trip up the mountain began. "Whenever it breaks!" came the reply.

Millions of people who would never entrust their lives to a frayed rope have entrusted their souls to themselves, or to a religious leader such as Buddha or Muhammad. In the end everyone has to trust somebody. The question is: Who has the most credibility? Which rope is most likely to hold in a crisis? Scan the horizons of history, study the works of the philosophers, investigate the claims of those who claim to be prophets of God. *To whom will you go?*

Our age prides itself in pluralism, the notion that every opinion is as valid as any other. There is no standard, we are told, by which morality and religion can be judged. All of these issues are simply a matter of personal preference.

Even within Christendom there are many denominations,

many competing beliefs, and each is presented as a viable option. Eastern religions are becoming popular here in the West, giving our nation even more alternatives that compete for the allegiance of men. Just as cable television gives viewers forty or fifty channels, so people today want to choose their own religion and moral beliefs from a wide variety of possibilities.

Subjectivism is king. Your choice of a religion or values is just as personal as walking into an ice cream parlor and choosing one of thirty-one different varieties. And just as you can mix and match your ice cream dish, so people take whatever they want from various beliefs and create their own special concoction. A smattering of Eastern religions along with some of Christ's words and the advice of a pop psychologist — all these are blended together into a private creed. Jacques Maritain said, "There are as many ways to approach God as there are wanderings on the earth or paths to His heart." So the message of today is, choose the path that's right for you.

This kind of eclecticism is not new. Men and women have often selected paths suited to their tastes and inclinations. Yes, even in the first century, the multitudes were confronted by a multiplicity of choices. The Greek world offered its philosophy and esoteric experiences; the Romans had their gods that promised political power. Various branches of Judaism all claimed to have the correct version of Abraham's religion. And when Christ appeared, He offered yet another choice — an unavoidable choice — to either accept Him or walk away.

If Peter was to be mightily used of God, he and the other disciples had to declare their unquestioned loyalty to the One whom they had come to know as the Messiah, the King. Peer pressure and the hatred of multitudes would be used as the hammer blows to test Peter's loyalty and commitment. If

Christ was who He claimed to be, competing loyalties would have to be uprooted from Peter's heart. Were he and the other disciples fully committed to Christ or not?

Christ providentially arranged an encounter that would force the disciples to make a choice. If any of them intended to desert their Master, they would be given that option. If they were wholly committed, they could affirm their love and determination. There would be no middle ground.

The background of this confrontation is found in John 6, where Christ took five loaves and two fish and fed a multitude. After this miracle we read, "Jesus therefore perceiving that they were intending to come and take Him by force, to make Him king, withdrew again to the mountain by Himself alone" (John 6:15). The crowd loved this man who could give them bread at a moment's notice. Little wonder they wanted Him to be King!

Christ was not misled by His popularity. In order to weed out the crowd, He made a series of statements that would prove that His admirers were quite disinterested in serious spiritual commitment. For example, He said, "No man can come to Me, unless the Father who sent Me draws him; and I will raise him up on the last day" (v. 44). The people were offended at the idea that they could not come to God on their own. The doctrine that we of ourselves cannot choose Christ was just as unpopular then as it is today.

To make matters worse, Christ made comments that were even more offensive. "Truly, truly I say to you, unless you eat the flesh of the Son of Man and drink His blood, you have no life in yourselves. He who eats My flesh and drinks My blood has eternal life; and I will raise him up at the last day. For My flesh is true food, and My blood is true drink" (vv. 53-55). These statements puzzled the multitude. They knew that cannibalism was inconsistent with the teachings of the Old Testament, which also taught that blood was not to be drunk. In what sense, therefore, should they be eating Christ's flesh and drinking His blood?

If they had listened more closely, they would have understood that Christ was not speaking literally, for He interprets His own words. "He who eats My flesh and drinks My blood abides in Me, and I in him. As the living Father sent Me, and I live because of the Father, so he who eats Me, he also shall live because of Me" (vv. 56-57). Christ was talking about a relationship with Him that is based on faith. Just as He lived in dependence upon the Father, so we are to live in dependence upon Him—that is what it means to eat His flesh and drink His blood. What physical bread is to the body, our union with Christ is to the soul. Then even more clearly Christ adds, "It is the Spirit who gives life; the flesh profits nothing; the words that I have spoken to you are spirit and are life" (v. 63).

Despite this explanation, an argument erupted in the crowd. They had followed Christ because He was able to give them physical bread, but they disdained His insistence that the spiritual bread from heaven was of primary importance. And at last we read, "As a result of this many of His disciples withdrew, and were not walking with Him any more" (v. 66). No matter how favorably they had felt about Jesus just the day before, they simply could not accept this teaching about their need for spiritual nourishment.

These "hard sayings" forced a moment of decision. Those who were spiritually hungry could ponder Christ's words and learn more about their need for heavenly bread. Those who cared only about physical bread would be bored with these spiritual insights. Thus Christ separated the grain from the chaff.

Though Christ knew that many people would leave Him, He still felt the hurt. He never accepted rejection without pain. Isaiah predicted, "He was despised and forsaken of men, a man of sorrows, and acquainted with grief; and like one from whom men hid their face, He was despised and we did not esteem Him" (Isa. 53:3).

Being forsaken was difficult, for He felt emotional distress. "Surely our griefs He Himself bore, and our sorrows He carried; yet we ourselves esteemed Him stricken, smitten of God, and afflicted" (v. 4). Jesus felt grief, pain, and loneliness.

As the crowd was dispersing in disappointment and anger, Jesus turned to the Twelve and said, "You do not want to go away also, do you?" (John 6:67) The question shows that Christ was hoping that the disciples would not join the fickle crowd. He was not disappointed.

This was one of Peter's finest moments. The Divine Sculptor was begetting results. Peter was becoming more committed to his Master; the transformation from Simon to Peter was gradual, but sure.

In the presence of the other disciples and within earshot of those in the crowd who cared to listen, Peter asked a question that should lodge like an arrow in every human heart: "Lord, to whom shall we go? You have words of eternal life. And we have believed and have come to know that You are the Holy One of God" (vv. 68-69). Peter was saying in effect, "The people might not like what You are saying . . . but what are our options? Who is a better teacher? Who is a better Savior? Who knows God better than You do? *There is nowhere else to go.*"

Christ has no rivals. Contrary to the pluralism of that day and of ours as well, religious truth is just as absolute as science or even mathematics. If Jesus Christ is right, all others are wrong. Just as one cannot walk in two directions simultaneously, so our hearts cannot be divided. Peter may not have been conscious of the implications of his remarks, but from him we can deduce that truth has these three characteristics:

Truth Is Consistent

Peter knew that if the crowds following Jesus were truly His disciples, they would be rejecting other religions and other authorities. To say *yes* to Christ was to say *no* to the Pharisees; to say *yes* to Christ was to say *no* to the esoteric religions that permeated the Middle East. *Christ's teaching was so unique, so different, that it could not be combined with the teachings of others.*

The different religions of the world cannot all be equally right! For example, Hindus believe that salvation means losing your personal identity, as a drop of water is lost in the ocean. Buddha began a new religion because he was dissatisfied with Hinduism and taught that salvation was a tortuous journey, dependent solely on human merit and suffering. Technically, Buddhists do not even believe in the existence of God, whereas Hindus have 330 million different gods! Muhammad taught that salvation came by obeying his teachings. His followers were to do what he said, not what he himself did, for his behavior contradicted his own teachings. Islam involves a complicated system of works that is quite different from the other religions mentioned.

There is a widespread assumption in America today that the religions of the world are essentially the same and only superficially different. However, the reverse is actually true: *the religions of the world are superficially the same but fundamentally different.* We shall see that Christianity is in a class by itself, with no real common ground with other teachings. The differences are radical, complete, and insurmountable.

Truth is always consistent with itself. If something is true, its opposite cannot also be true. It is not possible to combine the basic teachings of the world's religions without accepting mindless contradictions. Nor is there a basic core of so-called truth that unites the religions of the world.

When the disciples chose to follow Jesus, they turned their

backs on all rivals. If Christ was partly right and partly wrong, He was unworthy of their allegiance. Or if they were committed to Him and also to another prophet, they would be reducing Christ to the level of a fallible man. Either they had to accept all that Christ was and claimed to be, or else they had to reject Him. Unlike fallible men, Christ could not afford to be wrong, even once.

If Christ was the Son of the living God as Peter affirmed, He was in a class by Himself—perfect, holy, and totally reliable.

There is nowhere else to go.

Truth Is Universal

Peter said, "You have words of eternal life. And we have believed and have come to know that You are the Holy One of God" (vv. 68-69). Peter knew that truth was rooted in the nature of God and not subject to personal opinion. If Christ is indeed the Holy One of God and has the words of eternal life, His teachings are applicable to all the cultures of the world.

It is folly to suppose one can say that a particular religion is true for me but may not be true for you. Nor is there a religion that is right for one culture but wrong for another. Various ice cream options may be of equal value, but eternal truth is precious and unchangeable. When Christ said, "I am the way, and the truth, and the life; no one comes to the Father but through Me" (John 14:6), He was excluding all other avenues of approach to God.

It would be absurd to say that $2+2=4$ is only an American idea. Obviously, the same arithmetic holds true all over the world and is immune to change based on one's ethnic, cultural, or religious background. The truth that Christ came to proclaim is universal, applicable to all nations. Yes, religious truth is different from mathematics; but as we have seen, it is just as consistent, just as universal. Truth can never be based on a majority vote. Truth can be rejected by men and still remain unchanged. The crowds were turning away from Christ; His popularity was in sharp decline. Peter made this pledge of loyalty at a time when the tide was beginning to turn against Jesus. This is further proof that commitment to truth is often a lonely enterprise. Though the opinions of the crowds change, truth cannot.

Truth Is Rooted in Evidence

Most philosophers would agree that if religious truth did exist, it would be consistent and universal. But many would dispute the claim that such truth actually can be discovered. The question is: How do we know that Christ's particular claims are true? Peter added, "We . . . have come to know that You are the Holy One of God" (6:69). In the next chapter we shall see that Peter's understanding of Christ was granted to him by the Holy Spirit. Such a revelation is necessary because by nature our hearts are blinded, unwilling to see spiritual reality. This is so in part because we intuitively know that, if Christ is who He claims to be, we will be exposed for what we are in His presence. Another reason it is so is because we are basically dishonest when looking at evidence we don't like to see. As Christ taught, "No one can come to Me, unless it has been granted him from the Father" (v. 65).

Yet, quite apart from such a special work of God, the evidence for the authority of Christ, even taken by itself, is overwhelming. Those who believe in Christ have excellent historical and logical reasons to do so. True, we accept Christ by faith, but it is faith supported by evidence.

Why Christ? Why is He unique, separate from all the others? First of all, because of *what He did;* His miracles were observable, they were not a product of magic or fakery.

When He turned the water into wine, it was a visible miracle known by all at the feast. When He healed a nobleman's son, the man discovered that the moment of recovery coincided with Christ's healing word. And when Christ took five loaves and two fish and fed a multitude, everyone knew that this was not sleight of hand.

Eventually, He would die and be resurrected as further evidence that He was more than just the Son of a carpenter. The historical evidence for Christ's resurrection is so powerful that many skeptics have had to admit that the New Testament accounts are reliable.

Second, Christ is unique because of *what He taught*. Visualize a page with a column running down the middle. To the left we write all of the other religions of the world, and they all agree on one thing: One must earn merit to attain salvation. Whether it be Hinduism, Buddhism, Islam—human effort is always part of the salvation process. You can also put in this column those branches of Christendom that believe that salvation is a cooperative effort between God and man. God has done His part, we are told, now we must do ours!

In contrast, we must put the teachings of Christ in the right-hand column. Salvation, He taught, is a free gift given to those who believe in Him. No one else could make a sinless sacrifice, shedding His blood which is of infinite value to those who believe. "Truly, truly, I say to you, he who hears My word, and believes Him who sent Me, has eternal life, and does not come into judgment, but has passed out of death into life" (5:24).

Salvation *has* to be a free gift, because all human goodness falls short of God's holy standard. There is nothing we can do to make ourselves worthy of grace, or to accumulate merits whereby we might be saved. Even if salvation were 95 percent of God and 5 percent human effort, we could never be sure that we had done our part. If we are to enjoy an entrance into heaven at death, we must receive a gift that is unearned, wholly dependent on God's initiative and grace. Christ's ideas did not save us. His *death* was the act that made salvation available. This explains why Christ stands without peers amid the prophets and teachers of the world. He stands in opposition to everything the world believes. In some canyons in America two mountains may appear to be attached to one another. But as we get closer, we see that they are separated by a chasm. The towering banks go down for thousands of feet and never get near each other. And at the bottom they are separated by a dark, fast-moving, deep, and uncrossable river.

Appearances to the contrary, all attempts to link Christ with other teachers of religion are superficial and misleading. He is not just different from them, but *radically* different. There is no common ground, no bridge that unites Him with others. Christ, and Christ alone, presents salvation as a free gift of God given to helpless sinners.

Christ is also unique because of who He claimed to be. Think about His astounding claims. During the revolution of 1918 in what would become the Soviet Union, Lenin said that if communism were implemented there would be enough bread in every household. Yet he never had the nerve to say, "I am the bread of life; he who comes to Me shall not hunger, and he who believes in Me shall never thirst" (6:35).

Hitler made astounding claims for the role of Germany on Planet Earth, believing he was instigating a thousand-year *Reich* (rule). Despite his outlandish claims, he never said, "I am the way, and the truth, and the life; no one comes to the Father, but through Me" (14:6).

Buddha taught enlightenment, and yet died seeking more light. He never said, "I am the light of the world; he who follows Me shall not walk in the darkness, but shall have the light of life" (8:12).

New Age gurus assure us of the doctrine of reincarnation, saying we will be recycled until we "get it right." But they do not have the courage to say, "I am the resurrection and the life; he who believes in Me shall live even if he dies, and everyone who lives and believes in Me shall never die" (11:25-26).

Muhammad claimed that he and his tribes were descendants of Ishmael, another son of Abraham. But he did not say, "Truly, truly, I say to you, before Abraham was born, I AM" (8:58).

Freud believed that psychotherapy would heal people's emotional and spiritual pains. But he could not say, "Peace I leave with you; My peace I give to you; not as the world gives, do I give to you. Let not your heart be troubled, nor let it be fearful" (14:27).

Truth Must Be Accepted/Rejected

We all must go somewhere. Separated from God by our sin yet facing the prospect of living eternally, we all need help. Where do we go in our loneliness and pain? Where do we go with our unanswered questions? To whom shall we go when our own resources lead to despair? To education? To money? To science? To whom shall we go?

"A test of the value of any given thing is whether or not a substitute can be found for it," wrote Clarence McCartney. "If some other thing will serve just as well, then its value is limited. But if there is no substitute for it, it is of highest value" (*Peter and His Lord* [New York: Abingdon, Cokesbury, 1937], p. 42). No one else can take Christ's place; no one can do for us what He has done. There is nowhere else to go.

F.B. Meyer wrote:

To whom shall we go when in the light of the great

white throne we suddenly find that snow-water can never cleanse hearts and consciences, on which sin has laid its defiling hand?

To whom shall we go when one by one the lights which we have trusted die out in the sky and neither sun nor stars shine for many days, and no small tempest lies upon the distraught soul, which hears the breakers dashing on an unknown shore?

To whom shall we go in the loneliness of age, in the pains of mortal sickness, in the hour of death, in the day of account, amid the splendour of a holiness which angels cannot face, and a purity before which the heavens are not clean? (*Peter*, Revell, p. 52)

The skeptic will deride us, the ritualist will offer us a meaningful yet empty rite. The philosopher will give us the presumptions of fallible men. The moralist will give us the guidance which he himself cannot follow. Only Christ could say, "All things have been handed over to Me by My Father; and no one knows the Son, except the Father; nor does anyone know the Father, except the Son, and anyone to whom the Son wills to reveal Him" (Matt. 11:27).

Who has more insight into the nature of God than Christ? Who has made more astounding claims and then performed miracles to confirm them? What man on Planet Earth has ever spoken as has this One? Whose death can make atonement for our sins?

Somewhere I read:

To the baker, He is the Bread of Life.
To the banker, He is the Hidden Treasure.
To the florist, He is the Lily of the Valley.
To the astronomer, He is the Bright and Morning Star.
To the therapist, He is the Wonderful Counselor.

To the builder, He is the Chief Cornerstone.
To the philosopher, He is the Wisdom of God.
To the scientist, He is the Creator.
To the sinner, He is the Lamb of God.
To the politician, He is the King of kings.

To whom shall we go? There are no other options. "You have words of eternal life. And we have believed and have come to know that You are the Holy One of God."

There was one disciple who did not agree with Peter. He went somewhere else. He refused to see Christ as "the Holy One of God." Judas decided that he would turn to himself; he chose to make decisions based on what appeared to be his immediate, selfish needs. Though he listened to Peter's moving response, he only hardened his heart once again. Thus Christ responded to Peter's confession with these frightening words: "Did I Myself not choose you, the Twelve, and yet one of you is a devil?" (John 6:70)

Before Judas rejected what he heard, he should have made certain he could find someone else to take Christ's place. There is none other, of course. Hence Judas was eternally lost. We don't know all the reasons why Christ chose Judas, but doubtless Christ wanted to demonstrate that *even those who appear to serve with the highest honor may have an apostate heart.* Here was a man whose apostasy was concealed, but within time it would be revealed.

Judas was lost forever because he refused to accept Christ as his personal sin-bearer. For if one does not come to the Son of God, there is none other.

Peter knew that we all must go somewhere. We are not able to take away our own sin; we cannot bring ourselves to God.

Let us come quickly to Christ. There is *nowhere else to go.*

Chapter Five

THOU ART THE CHRIST

(Read Matthew 16:13-28)

Christ knew that the eternal destiny of all men was dependent on their relationship with Him. Though He was honored for His miracles and teachings, only those who understood that He was the Messiah, the Son of God, could benefit from the work He came to do. For this reason He kept pressing men and women to make up their minds about Him.

Though Peter had already recognized Him as "the Holy One of God," Christ kept probing his mind and heart. He also wanted the other disciples to clarify their own understanding of His person and work. The Sculptor was cutting away any misgivings His disciples had. The choice was clear: If He is God in the flesh, serve Him; if He is anything less, consider Him only of passing interest.

Jesus was in the area of Caesarea Philippi, north of Galilee, about six months away from going to Jerusalem to die. Here at the base of a mountain (most likely Mount Hermon), He asked His disciples a series of questions that would force them to clarify their understanding of Him. He was not taking an opinion poll, nor did He ask these questions because He was seeking information for His own good. Just as God the Father asked Adam and Eve a question in the Garden of Eden for their benefit, so Christ asked the disciples questions as a part of their learning process.

"Now when Jesus came into the district of Caesarea Philippi, He began asking His disciples, saying, 'Who do people say that the Son of Man is?' And they said, 'Some say John the Baptist; some, Elijah; and others, Jeremiah, or one of the prophets' " (Matt. 16:13-14).

Missing is any reference to Christ as the Messiah. Months earlier multitudes appeared to be convinced that Christ was the promised One, but opposition to Him was beginning to build. If some common people had such convictions, they were afraid to share them. Or possibly they had become convinced that their original opinion of Him was mistaken.

However, we must also remember popular opinion held that the Messiah would be a resurrected figure from the past. This would explain why John the Baptist and several heroes of bygone days were included in this list of possible candidates. Thus, some in the crowd may have believed that Christ was the Messiah, but nevertheless thought He had had a past existence.

Why would some think He was John the Baptist? This rumor began with King Herod who had murdered John the Baptist. Recall that the king had put John in prison because the prophet had boldly told him that it was not lawful for him to take his brother's wife. He married her anyway and when the daughter of his new wife danced at a party, Herod promised her anything she would ask, up to half of his kingdom. Her mother, now in the king's court, was so incensed about John the Baptist's petty moral judgments that she requested his head. To please his new bride and to save face, Herod had John executed (14:2-12).

Understandably, the king had some sleepless nights about this shameless murder and was haunted by the possibility that John might rise from the dead. Christ's miracles made him think that this dreaded possibility had come true. When word reached him about the activities of Christ, he said, "This is John the Baptist; he has risen from the dead; and that is why miraculous powers are at work in him" (v. 2). So the rumor circulated among the masses: This is John the Baptist.

Others said Christ was Elijah. This was based on a prophecy in the last chapter of the Old Testament: "Behold, I am going to send you Elijah the prophet before the coming of the great and terrible day of the Lord" (Mal. 4:5). Many believed that Elijah would literally return.

If they had paid close attention, they would have realized that John the Baptist was the fulfillment of this prophecy. He was not the reincarnation of Elijah, but he had a similar ministry. The explanation of this prophecy is found in the words of an angel to John's father Zacharias: "And it is he who will go as a forerunner before Him in the spirit and power of Elijah" (Luke 1:17). Yes, in this sense Elijah had come, but they didn't realize it.

Others said Jesus was Jeremiah, the weeping prophet. Jeremiah wept over Jerusalem, just as Jesus would do shortly. Or, He might be one of the other prophets.

The people of Christ's day made some willful mistakes in understanding Him. They should have seen His miracles, heard His sermons, and come to a better conclusion. But many in our day, despite the advantages of education and a more privileged perspective, have equally confused beliefs regarding Christ.

Christ cannot be ignored. Whether in this life or the next, all men will eventually find themselves in His presence, with Him either as Savior or as Judge. Ultimately, everyone has to make up his or her mind about Him. The masses in Christ's day gave their response. He had, however, one more question to ask.

Peter's Personal Conviction

Like an arrow aimed for its intended target, Jesus now turned to His disciples and asked a pertinent personal question: "But who do you say that I am?" And Peter, ever the first to speak, answered magnificently, "Thou art the Christ, the Son of the living God" (Matt. 16:16). We should not think that only now Peter had reached this conclusion. He had made similar statements before (see chap. 4). But never before had he stated his conclusion so clearly, so briefly, so memorably.

Peter, I am sure, was speaking for all of the disciples, but his answer must be seen primarily as his own heartfelt conviction. He knew that the name *Christ* meant the "Anointed One." He recognized that this Man was the Christ who was the fulfillment of the Old Testament predictions. He was the Prophet, Priest, and King.

The phrase, "Son of the living God," refers to Christ as the special, only begotten Son of God. When Christ spoke of Himself as a Son and God as His Father, the Jews accused Him of blasphemy, making Himself equal with God (John 5:18). They understood that this kind of sonship implied equality with God. Christ's sonship does not refer to *time*, but to *rank*. God the Father did not exist before God the Son. Both the Son and the Father existed from all eternity. Christ is the unique One, the God-man.

By asking the disciples this question, Jesus brought Peter's faith to its clearest public expression. Here, for all to see, was the earnest response of his heart. This was another one of Peter's finest moments.

Jesus continued, "And I also say to you that you are Peter, and upon this rock I will build My church; and the gates of Hades shall not overpower it" (Matt. 16:18). This is the only prediction Christ made about the establishment of His church, a prophecy that was fulfilled on the Day of Pentecost. This is the church of which He is the head, the church for which He died, and the church for which He will someday return.

In responding to Peter's ringing affirmation, Christ used the occasion to describe the church He is about to build. Notice these features: First, *Christ owns the church.* If Peter, or any one of us for that matter, should ever use the church as a platform to enhance our own careers, if we should ever treat the people of the church as if they belong to us, we are callously usurping an ownership which belongs to Christ alone. He purchased the church at high cost. It belongs to Him.

Second, *He builds the church.* He builds the church by granting eternal life to those who were chosen from before the foundation of the world. Then He gives each of its members spiritual gifts so that the ministry might flourish. When Cromwell ruled in England, he sent a delegation throughout the land searching for silver so that he could mint coins. His men returned to say that virtually all of the silver was contained in the statues within the churches. Cromwell is said to have replied, "Melt down the saints and put them into circulation!"

For 2,000 years the church has survived despite persecution, scandal, and heresy. Christ has, however, sustained the church He promised to build. Though the numbers have been comparatively small, the cause of Christ has triumphed in the world. The power of the church is unleashed when the saints are put into circulation, fulfilling their God-given responsibilities. And, in the end, the purposes of God will be clearly demonstrated.

Third, *Christ empowers the church,* for, "the gates of hades shall not overpower it." This expression, taken from the Book of Isaiah, is most probably a reference to death, specifically Christ's own death. He is warning the disciples that though He will pass through the iron gates of death, this will not mean that His church will come to an end. Indeed, as the disciples would later understand, His death was necessary to establish the church.

Peter's dramatic confession initiated a moving response from Christ, a personal affirmation that the church was about to be built. And Peter would play a leading role in the drama.

When Augustine heard that Rome had been sacked, he was sorrowful but is quoted as saying, "Whatever men build, men will destroy. Let's get on with building the kingdom of God!" Yes, men will destroy what they build, but what God builds will endure.

Peter's Personal Promise
The sand dune had become a rock.

"Blessed are you, Simon Barjona, because flesh and blood did not reveal this to you, but My Father who is in heaven. And I also say to you that you are Peter, and upon this rock I will build My church; and the gates of Hades shall not over-power it" (vv. 17-18).

Jesus refers to Peter as "Simon Barjona," just as He did in that first encounter along the banks of the Jordan River. That prediction is now fulfilled as Christ makes the change in names official. The shifting sand had become a rock. And it would be on a rock that the church would be built.

Two controversial questions have been associated with this text. First, what did Christ mean when He said that His church would be built on "this rock"? And second, what "keys" were given to Peter? (v. 19)

Oscar Cullman, who has made an exhaustive study of Peter's life and ministry, says, "Until the beginning of the third century it never occurred to a single Bishop of Rome to refer the saying of Matthew 16:17ff to himself in the sense of headship of the entire Church" *(Peter* [Philadelphia: Westminster Press, 1953], p. 234). For example, Chrysostom believed that the rock meant Peter's confession of faith, and Augustine taught that Jesus was referring to Himself and not Peter.

When Pope Leo I wanted to enhance his credibility as he faced opposition from rival Constantinople, he appealed to the primacy of the Roman Church based on this statement of Christ to Peter. The argument was that Peter was the first bishop of Rome, and since the church was built on him, the succession of the Roman papacy was justified.

Greek scholars have pointed out that there are two words for "rock" used here. "You are *Petros* [a piece of rock] and upon this *petra* [a slab of rock] I will build My church." This would suggest that Christ was not referring to Peter but to Himself. The Apostle Paul spoke of Christ as the rock: "For no man can lay a foundation other than the one which is laid, which is Jesus Christ" (1 Cor. 3:11).

A second possibility is that Christ was referring to Peter's *confession* as the rock upon which the church would be built. On the rock of the deity of Christ—on the rock of His unique position as God's special Son—on this rock the future work of His kingdom would rest.

A third interpretation is that Christ indeed did refer to Peter. Since he had confessed Christ in the presence of the other apostles, Christ was now conferring upon him a special place in the coming church. Peter was, as it were, the first stone in the new building. He was closest to the foundation stone, namely Christ Himself. Years later the Apostle Paul spoke of the apostles and prophets as being a part of the foundation of the church, "Having been built upon the foundation of the apostles and prophets, Christ Jesus Himself being the Cornerstone" (Eph. 2:20). Peter is one important stone among many in the building of this spiritual edifice.

This interpretation would also agree with Peter himself, who spoke of Christ as the Cornerstone and all of us as "living stones" in the building (1 Peter 2:4-8). Peter and the other apostles are next to the Chief Cornerstone, then follows the entire redeemed host. As we shall see, Peter preached both to Jews and Gentiles, playing a crucial role in the establishment of the church. The rest of us are also there, a part of the structure, living stones in Christ's building.

This text, however, cannot be used to justify the papacy as it has been known throughout history. Even if the church was built on Peter alone, (1) nowhere do we read that Peter's authority is transferable; and, (2) we have no warrant to suppose that this authority has been transferred to the popes of Rome; and finally, (3) although Peter may have come to Rome near the end of his life, there is no historical evidence whatever that he was the bishop of Rome.

A second crucial question: What are the keys which were given to Peter? "I will give you the keys of the kingdom of heaven; and whatever you shall bind on earth shall have been bound in heaven, and whatever you shall loose on earth shall have been loosed in heaven" (Matt. 16:19). Though the words were spoken to Peter, we know that all of the disciples shared the responsibility as keepers of the keys. In Matthew 18:18, Christ gave the responsibility of binding and loosing to all the disciples.

A key is used to open a door or to close it. Thus the apostles and especially Peter will open the kingdom of heaven to new groups of people. On the Day of Pentecost, Peter opened the door of the church to the Jews when 3,000 responded to his message of repentance. Later he opened the door to the Gentiles when in obedience to Christ he went to Joppa and shared the Gospel with Cornelius and his household (Acts 10).

Keys not only have the power to open doors but also to

close them. Those who repent can be admitted, but those who are unrepentant can also be excluded. Unfortunately, as the centuries progressed and the church itself slipped into apostasy, it began to exclude the very people of God who should have been welcomed into the church! Such is the nature of man that the pure Gospel of grace was soon perverted (particularly after the time of Constantine) so that the genuine believers found themselves outside of the official established church. The heretics within were administering severe discipline (often torture and death) to the saints without.

This text has often been interpreted to mean that men on earth have the power to determine God's actions in heaven. The theory is that when we bind or loose individuals, God binds or looses these same people. God, it is thought, follows our lead.

But notice the tense of the verbs in the verse: "Whatever you shall bind on earth *shall have been bound* in heaven, and whatever you loose on earth *shall have been loosed* in heaven" (Matt. 16:19, italics mine). Men can only do what has already been accomplished in heaven. We do not direct God; God directs us.

Properly understood, the church today can still exercise the responsibility of administering the "keys" by welcoming sinners into the church, affirming that if they accept the Gospel of God's grace they will be saved. On the other hand, we can also exclude from fellowship those who know the truth but will not abide by its teachings. We do this only because, according to God's Word, He has already done this in heaven.

Thankfully, the souls of men and women are in the hands of God, not men. Those whom God has included in His church no man can exclude. Even if men should err, what God has done still stands.

Peter's Personal Revelation

Let's consider once more Christ's words, "Blessed are you, Simon Barjona, because flesh and blood did not reveal this to you, but My Father who is in heaven" (v. 17). Where did Peter's clear faith come from? Was it inherent within his own nature, just waiting to be drawn out at the right moment? Was Peter's conclusion the result of careful thought and human investigation? No, the origin of Peter's faith was not flesh and blood, but a revelation from the Father. All the natural endowments of human nature could never have produced this theological insight. His statement was the result of *a miracle of personal enlightenment.*

God was the origin of Peter's faith. Peter was not mouthing the words of a creed nor even drawing some legitimate conclusions based on his careful observation. This was a faith wrought in the depths of his being as a gift of God. It was a faith that was personal and final. Nothing except a revelation from God can give us a view of Christ that fills our hearts with adoring wonder. The darkness can only be dispelled by a miracle, a shaft of divine light. *To cure our spiritual blindness is a divine work.*

The great German preacher Helmut Thielicke tells how on a cycling tour of southern Germany he came to a village at midmorning, ravenously hungry because he had missed breakfast. To his delight he saw a shop window in the village street with a notice, "Hot Rolls." With his gastric juices flowing in eager anticipation, he went inside only to discover that the shop sold no rolls, either hot or cold. It was a print shop; the sign on the outside was simply an example of the kind of lettering the shop could produce.

So it is with those who use words but neither understand nor trust their meaning. Think of the millions who have recited the words of a creed affirming the divinity of Christ and yet are eternally lost. The words may be true, but personal affirmation is needed before they are applied. Like a sign on a window, letters can just be glued on the outer shell of an empty spiritual life.

Stand at any major intersection in the United States and ask, "Who is Jesus Christ?" and you will receive many answers that appear to be complimentary. Christ will be honored for being a great teacher, for living by the Golden Rule, and for preaching the love of God. He will be praised for many virtues, admired for His humility, and remembered for His kindness to the poor. Some will commend Him for turning water into wine and criticizing the established religion of the day.

Laudable though such responses appear to be, they are an insult. If that is all Jesus was, He was a liar. Remember this basic axiom: *The better the world understands the biblical Christ, the more it hates Him.* If they speak well of Him, it is because they do not understand Him. Those secular musicals, movies, and books that are favorable to Christ inevitably misunderstand His message. Alexander Maclaren understood with clarity. "What we believe to be precious it [the world] regards as of no account. What we believe to be fundamental truth, it passes by as of little importance. Much which we feel to be wrong, it regards as good. Our tools are its tinsel, and its jewels are our tinsel" *(With Christ in the Upper Room* [Grand Rapids: Baker, 1956], p. 225).

Only when Christ stays at a safe distance, preferably in a manger, does the world feel comfortable in His presence. When confronted with His deity and holiness; when confronted with its own sinfulness in His presence; the world then flees to its own opinions and excuses. To confess Christ fully is indeed a gracious gift of God.

Benjamin Franklin was a great friend of the revivalist, George Whitefield. Yet before he died, Franklin said that although Whitefield had often prayed for his conversion, the revivalist "did not have the satisfaction of having his prayers answered." And when asked by Ezra Stiles, the president of Yale University, whether he believed in the deity of Christ, Franklin said he had doubts about that doctrine, though he "soon would have the opportunity of knowing the truth with less trouble."

Pity Franklin! Imagine dying without knowing that Christ is indeed the Messiah, the Son of the living God. Imagine dying and being forced to stand before God on the basis of one's own flawed performance.

What do *you* think of Christ?

Chapter Six

THE HIGH COST
OF AVOIDING THE CROSS

(Read Matthew 16:21-28)

The cross is a symbol of Christianity, though I fear it has lost its meaning. In our culture the cross has become a medallion that may be worn on a necklace or bracelet. Or it is an architectural wonder that adorns our church buildings. The cross is an ornament, rather than an instrument of death. We have romanticized it and erased its terror. And its power!

Today the electrocution of criminals or the use of a gas chamber is considered by many to be "cruel and unusual punishment." But in Christ's time, criminals were nailed to a stout trunk of a tree with a rough branch as a crosspiece. Rusty nails and pieces of rope were used to hold victims on the beams while they writhed for days before they died. Cicero said that the victims often became raving maniacs and had their tongues cut out so that people would not have to listen to their vain and piercing babbling.

Yes, the cross is the symbol of Christianity, and our relationship to it determines our eternal destiny. But let us never forget that the cross in and of itself was an instrument of torture, a summons to death. There Christ hung for us, and He invites us to follow Him.

Peter needed to learn the meaning of the cross. He would have to understand why Christ had to die such a horrible death. Later he would be told that he would die in a similar way, following His Master. The cross would be the chisel used to put the final touches on a life being molded by God.

Peter might well have felt a rush of confidence when Jesus commended him for his spiritual insight. "Thou art the Christ, the Son of the living God." Think of the encouragement he received when he heard his Master say, *"Blessed are you, Simon Barjona, because flesh and blood did not reveal this to you, but My Father who is in heaven."* Then Jesus went on to tell him that he would play a major role in the establishment of the church.

This was surely Peter's happiest day.

It was also one of his saddest days.

Christ's Perspective

Like a squall rising in the noonday sun, Christ interrupted His disciples' joyous mood with a word of warning and a dire prediction about the days ahead: *"Then He warned the disciples that they should tell no one that He was the Christ"* (Matt. 16:20). Why this command? We would expect that Christ would encourage them to make Him known far and wide. But His disciples did not yet have a full understanding of His message; they understood His person, but they were unclear about the work the Messiah had come to do. They knew that the Messiah was to reign; they didn't know that He was to die. They thought of the crown, but not of the cross. If they had told what they knew, the wrong message would have spread throughout the land.

Then came the bombshell: *"From that time Jesus began to show His disciples that He must go to Jerusalem, and suffer many things from the elders and chief priests and scribes, and be killed, and be raised up on the third day"* (v. 21). Notice the details: (1) He must go to Jerusalem, for Jerusalem is the city of sacrifice; and, (2) He must suffer at the hands of the elders and chief priests, the very ones who were venerated in Israel. This group of men, known as the Sanhedrin, were the most learned and envied of all the leaders. Though representing the official religion of the time, they were the most hostile to Christ. Then, (3) He had to die and be raised again. Previously He had hinted that this would happen, but now it was made perfectly clear. No other option was under consideration. Despite the horror that awaited Him, *this had to be.*

If Christ had been a false messiah bent on staging a messianic coup, He certainly would not have chosen to go to Jerusalem to die. He would have taken pains to fulfill the popular messianic expectations of the day, namely to stage a revolt against Roman occupation. The fact that He countered public opinion at almost every point confirms His authenticity. And it clarified the public's mistaken notions about the coming kingdom.

Why didn't the Jews understand Christ's predictions that the Messiah would first have to suffer, before coming in glory? Our eyes often see only what we want to see. The idea of a Messiah ruling in uninterrupted glory was appealing. The people of the day were more preoccupied with the political bondage of Rome than with the spiritual bondage of their own sin. Who wants a Messiah who will be humiliated on a cross?

Christ wanted to prepare them for the sorrow that awaited them. The calendar of events was clear, certain, and uncompromising. He wanted them to understand that His death was ordained; it was not a terrible tragedy that had caught the Almighty off guard. Indeed, no matter how excruciating the days ahead, all of this was a part of the divine purpose.

After Christ's ascension, Peter would see all of this with clarity. While leading a prayer meeting after being jailed and beaten, Peter affirmed that various groups had cooperated to crucify Christ, *"to do whatever Thy hand and Thy purpose pre-*

destined to occur" (Acts 4:28). No guesswork here! God's will had been done!

As for now, Peter simply could not see how the cross could be a part of God's plan. When Christ gave details about His impending death, Peter objected. The man who worshiped Christ found himself reprimanding Him!

Peter's Perspective

Peter found Christ's statement so staggering that he thought he should use his newfound honor to actually rebuke his Master. For all of his spiritual insight, he simply could not fathom why Christ, his Messiah, would have to subject Himself to such humiliation. Why would Christ have to die? And even if He had to die, why would it be so shamefully?

"And Peter took Him aside and began to rebuke Him, saying, 'God forbid it, Lord! This shall never happen to You'" (Matt. 16:22). To spare his Master a public admonition, Peter took Jesus aside privately and told Him that this prediction simply was unacceptable. He deeply loved the Lord and had His best interests in mind. The thought of seeing his Master suffer such a death was simply too much.

Often well-meaning friends give us unscriptural and harmful advice! Sometimes we have been encouraged to rationalize our disobedience by listening to those who love us but lack wisdom. Perhaps we've broken promises, tolerated secret sin, or told a lie, all because obedience seemed so painful. Our friends who don't want to see us suffer have encouraged us to avoid the painful duty that lay in our path.

Peter's reasoning is understandable; it seemed so inappropriate that the Son of God should be so grossly humiliated. How can a divine Christ die? If He is the Son of God, King, and Messiah—how can He also be a helpless victim, shamefully nailed to a cross? To put it in a logical form, "If A is true, B can't be true," Peter must have thought.

Obviously there is nothing wrong with human logic if the premises are correct. But Peter was making assumptions beyond his realm of expertise! What made him so sure that a Messiah could not die; or, more pointedly, what made him so sure that a Messiah was not *supposed* to die?

We stand in awe of this encounter. Peter, the one who loved Jesus supremely, becomes the very one who stands in the way of Christ's obedience! Peter, with love flowing in his heart for his Master, is now an instrument of Satan!

Peter's suggestion struck at the heart of God's everlasting covenant. The cross was predetermined to be the hinge on which God's purpose for mankind would turn. Without it there would be no removal of sin, no redemption. And now Peter stood between Jesus and His cross!

Clearly, Peter did not realize that by encouraging Christ to cancel Easter, *he was making his own salvation impossible!* If Christ had taken Peter's suggestion, Peter, like all the rest of us, would have been lost forever. For there outside Jerusalem's city walls, Christ would hang naked as the Sin-bearer for those who believe. Without the cross, there could be no crown.

Peter rebuked Jesus, but now he in turn was rebuked. Jesus told him that his suggestion was satanic! The best of motives can be no substitute for obedience to the will of God, even when that plan includes suffering.

The Father's Perspective

Where had Peter erred in his thinking? Why did he prove himself to be so fallible? Christ set the record straight: "But He turned and said to Peter, 'Get thee behind Me, Satan! You are a stumbling block to Me; for you are not setting your mind on God's interests, but man's' " (v. 23). Peter the rock had become a stone over which Christ was tempted to stumble! Unknowingly, Peter had laid a satanic snare for

Christ! Rather than acting like a disciple of his Master, he had become a tool of the devil! The man who spoke so eloquently under the inspiration of the Spirit of Light, now spoke under the compulsion of the spirit of darkness! He who had had a revelation from heaven, now had a revelation from hell!

Notice that Christ rebuked Satan, not Peter. He did not say, "Peter, get behind Me!" Such a rebuke would have made Peter withdraw from Christ's presence, permanently devastated. No, Christ saw Peter being used by the devil, and the origin of his suggestion had to be exposed. Thankfully, though Peter also bore responsibility, he will not be condemned along with the devil.

Christ did not mean that Peter was possessed by Satan. He meant that Peter's supposed wisdom and the devil's plan had coincided. Incredibly, the devil himself had already given the same advice to Christ! There on a high mountain, the tempter said to the Son of God, "All these things will I give You, if You fall down and worship me" (4:9). Satan told Christ He could have all the kingdoms of the world without dying. And now the voice of Christ's apostle sounded the same as the voice of the devil. *The voice of hate and the voice of misguided love were in unison.*

Indeed, Satan is able to put ideas into our minds that we think are our own. And so, through deception, the one who had just been declared to be a rock now became a stumbling block. The one who was to help Christ build His church now stood in the way of the God-ordained blueprint.

How did this happen? Christ explained, "You are not setting your mind on God's interests but man's." We should not be surprised that Peter could speak in league with an unholy spirit. We also have within ourselves that kind of ambiguity, that mixture of good and evil. We can rejoice in Christ during a church service and moments afterward be mean, filled with anger and venom. The same mouths that sing the songs of Zion can be used to gossip, demean, and deny Christ.

James marveled at the deceptiveness of the tongue: "But no one can tame the tongue; it is a restless evil and full of deadly poison. With it we bless our Lord and Father; and with it we curse men, who have been made in the likeness of God; from the same mouth come both blessing and cursing. My brethren, these things ought not to be this way" (James 3:8-10). Although in nature the same stream does not send forth both fresh water and bitter, James emphasizes that the tongue has this incredible capacity.

Jesus confronted the suggestion of His beloved disciple just as He confronted the words of Satan when tempted in the wilderness. Whether a temptation comes from the mouth of an angry devil or the mouth of a loving disciple, the final result is the same. In both instances the only appropriate response is, "Get thee behind Me!" Disobedience cannot substitute for obedience, even if done with the highest motives.

Our Perspective

Peter's desire to avoid the cross was intended to spare Christ a shameful death. He was by no means the last to diminish the cross. Our society, yes, even our evangelical churches minimize the cross in ways that are more subtle, but just as devastating.

How can we cheapen the cross? (1) By thinking that we must do some penance before we come to the cross to be forgiven. Often people feel that guilt is necessary, because we don't deserve to receive Christ's forgiveness. The purpose of guilt is to lead us to the cross; but once we have been there, guilt is *not* one of the ways in which God disciplines His people. Often we lose sight of the wonder of the cross and we bear our own guilt, forgetting that the sin troubling us is the sin that has already been taken away!

Then, (2) we can diminish the cross by thinking that we have committed a sin too big for God to forgive. Recently I received a letter from a man who had raped several women. In prison he came to accept Christ as his Savior. Though he mentally knows he is forgiven, his emotions will often not let him enjoy his forgiveness. He remembers the painful thought that his salvation has not changed the horrible consequences in the lives of his victims. Can such a one be forgiven? The answer is *yes!* Let us never minimize the cross by suggesting that some sins are unforgivable!

(3) We can minimize the cross by thinking that it is irrelevant to Christian victory. But Jesus went on to say to the disciples, "If anyone wishes to come after Me, let him deny himself and take up his cross and follow Me" (Matt. 16:24). Elsewhere He taught, "Truly, truly, I say to you, unless a grain of wheat falls into the earth and dies, it remains by itself alone; but if it dies, it bears much fruit" (John 12:24).

To take up our cross does not mean that we live with bad health, an irritable marriage partner, or some other calamity. Those kinds of crosses are common to all people in the world. To carry our cross for Christ means the renunciation of self-will; it means that we give up all attempts to be the center of our own life. To carry our cross means that we humbly submit to the supremacy of Christ. We have to be willing to be identified with Him even at great personal cost.

Finally, (4) the cross can be nullified by those who think there are other ways of salvation. As often as I can I witness to people, sharing the Good News. But from time to time I meet those who honestly tell me that they do not need Jesus! They see no reason to be saved from the wrath to come.

As we have learned, Christianity is only superficially the same as other religions. Many other religions offer blood to God for sin; in Christianity *God supplies the blood!* And the blood of the cross is the only blood He will accept. All other attempts to reach God diminish the wonder and the beauty of the cross, the only path to the Father.

Perhaps you have heard the story of the man who operated a drawbridge for a train. As the train was approaching, he began to lower the bridge, so that it would be entirely horizontal by the time the train approached. But as the bridge began its descent, he noticed that his own son was caught in between the gears. Instantly he had to choose; to save his son would mean that the train would be derailed and hundreds of people killed. With inexpressible anguish, he continued to lower the bridge, crushing his son beneath its weight. That day as the train sped across the bridge, people waved at the watchman, not knowing how much they owed him!

Today people go merrily on their way, forgetting that they owe God so very much! They have forgotten that His Son was sacrificed so that we might live. "But may it never be that I should boast, except in the cross of our Lord Jesus Christ, through which the world has been crucified to me, and I to the world" (Gal. 6:14).

Although Christ spoke to Peter and Satan as if they were one, they were treated separately. Peter eventually turned and stood before Christ's face. Satan fled behind Christ's back. Peter could stand before his Lord once more, worthy of His name. This strong rebuke rescued Peter from the snare of the devil. The sharp chisel had exposed the fallacy of relying on human wisdom. Grace and judgment met together in the steady hand of the Master Sculptor.

In one day Peter was shaped by a wonderful affirmation and promise. . . . He was also shaped by a searing rebuke. Both were needed to chisel a rough stone, so that he would become a man of God.

With Peter we must learn the cross precedes the crown.

Chapter Seven

ONE WITH THE SOVEREIGN MASTER

(Read Matthew 17:24-27)

The fear of poverty has plagued every generation. A chosen few are born into wealth or have the good fortune to accumulate considerable riches, but the rest of mankind lives with the suspicion that they eventually will be abandoned to the fate of hunger and homelessness. Even Christians wonder whether God can be trusted to meet their needs.

Christ's disciples had their doubts too. At His command, they abandoned their vocations to wander around the land of Israel, following the steps of their Master. Some of their relatives and friends must have thought that such dedication to Christ was foolish. Why would anyone leave a job with a predictable income to live with a man who had no home, few clothes, and virtually no visible means of support?

Time and again the disciples had to relearn an important lesson: *When God calls, He supplies.* Their responsibility was to follow; His responsibility was to provide.

Missionaries are not the only ones in the school of faith. Most of us have been strategically placed in circumstances in which we are forced to believe God. Faith usually cannot be developed in an environment of ease; it can only flourish in an environment of hardship. Faith grows only when great faith is called for. Sadly, only the desperate believe.

Satan says, "Follow me and you will be rich." Christ makes no promises for wealth in this life, but assures us of the glory of the world to come. Whatever we give up to follow Him will be made up to us tenfold; He simply will not be outdone.

Peter had to learn this lesson many times. To be a man of faith, he had to draw from a well of experience. His qualifications as a future leader would depend on a reservoir of personal testing that would give him credibility. And so the Divine Sculptor would continue to shape the emerging form of this important leader.

Here we have one of the most interesting miracles Christ performed. Though it teaches us Christ's care for His disciples, it also is a lesson in responsibility and divine partnership. And, as is so often the case, Peter is in the middle of it all.

Here is the intriguing story:

And when they had come to Capernaum, those who collected the two-drachma tax came to Peter, and said, "Does your teacher not pay the two-drachma tax?" He said, "Yes." And when he came into the house, Jesus spoke to him first, saying, "What do you think, Simon? From whom do the kings of the earth collect customs or poll-tax, from their sons or from strangers?" And upon his saying, "From strangers," Jesus said to him, "Consequently the sons are exempt. But lest we give them offense, go to the sea, and throw in a hook, and take the first fish that comes up; and when you open its mouth, you will find a stater. Take that and give it to them for you and Me" (Matt. 17:24-27).

Nothing is sure, it is said, but death and taxes. Even our Lord was hounded by those who taxed the populace. This was not a civil tax, but a religious tax, used to pay for the ongoing ministries of the temple. This tax was introduced in Exodus 30:13: "This is what everyone who is numbered shall give: half a shekel according to the shekel of the sanctuary (the shekel is twenty gerahs), half a shekel as a contribution to the Lord." The temple services demanded a large sum of money: Sacrifices, incense, and the upkeep of the buildings was a costly business. Although this tax was voluntary, it was paid by those who felt an obligation to help continue the prescribed religious ceremonies.

How much was a half-shekel? If we think of the shekel as a dollar, we can think of a drachma as a quarter (four drachma make a shekel). Since a drachma was equivalent to approximately one day's wage, the average worker would have to work four days for a shekel. Of course half a shekel would be two drachma, or about two days' wage.

A tax collector visited the city of Capernaum, hoping to canvas the area, confronting men, urging them to pay this tax. The tax collector found Peter outside of the house (probably Peter's own house in the city) and asked: "Does your teacher not pay the two-drachma tax?" The question was phrased in such a way as to make it seem reasonable that no teacher would try to escape from this obligation.

Peter did not go into the house to consult with Christ. He answered for His Master, "Yes." And with that he walked into the house where Christ was, but before he could open his mouth, Christ (who knew what had been said outside) immediately replied, "What do you think, Simon? From whom do the kings of the earth collect customs or poll-tax, from their sons or from strangers?" (Matt. 17:25)

Peter correctly replied, "From strangers." Christ agreed, saying that this means that He, the Son of the Most High God, was under no obligation to pay taxes. But then He added, "But lest we give them offense, go to the sea, and throw in a hook, and take the first fish that comes up; and when you open its mouth, you will find a stater [a shekel coin]. Take that and give it to them for you and Me."

Not everyone believes that this story should be understood literally. William Barclay thinks that it would be immoral for Christ to encourage laziness by supplying money in such a miraculous way. He thinks that Christ was, in effect, saying, "Yes, Peter. You're right. We too, must pay our just and lawful debts. Well, you know how to do it. Back you go to the fishing for the day. You'll get plenty of money in the fishes' mouths to pay your dues! A day at the fishing will soon produce all we need" (*The Gospel of Matthew*, Vol. 2 [Edinburgh: St. Andrew's Press, 1957], p. 190).

God usually does supply money through our hard work rather than through a miraculous happenstance such as finding a coin in an unlikely place. And yes, if Peter had gone back to fishing for a day, he would have made enough money to pay the tax. But the text is rather clear: Christ told Peter that the first fish he would catch would have a shekel in its mouth, just enough to meet both of their obligations. Perhaps Christ is not teaching laziness, but rather teaching Peter (along with the rest of us) something about Himself and His care for His followers.

What does this story teach us about Jesus?

Christ's Sovereign Knowledge
Christ was totally in control of the situation. As already explained, He was inside the house when the conversation between the tax collector and Peter took place *outside*. And yet when Peter came into the house we read, "Jesus spoke to him first." Christ's question proved that He had full knowledge of the verbal give-and-take that took place outside.

Isaiah wrote, "It will also come to pass that before they call, I will answer; and while they are still speaking, I will hear" (Isa. 65:24). Christ has His eyes riveted completely upon us. The conversations whispered behind our backs; the thoughts that never give birth to words; the pain of relationships that will be ruptured in the future—all of this is already known to Him.

A college professor was sitting at his desk, correcting examination papers just turned in by a very large class. He glared from behind the tall stack of papers just as the last student approached him, paper in hand. The student had gone fifteen minutes beyond the time limit, so the professor with a wave of the hand rejected the student's paper. But the student drew himself up to full stature and asked, "Do you know who I am?" The professor replied, "No, how do you expect me to know the names of all 115 students in this class?" Whereupon the student quickly stuffed his paper into the middle of the big stack!

Though it is possible to take advantage of the limited knowledge of a professor, Jesus knows who we are. He knows what we are trying to hide; He knows what others are trying to hide from us. His knowledge encompasses the universe. Scientists teach us that the same basic elements used to make the stars are the building blocks from which our bodies are constructed. Understandably so, because they have the same Creator. In the same breath David speaks of both the physical universe and human experience as a part of God's unerring providence. In Psalm 147:3-5 we read, "He heals the brokenhearted, and binds up their wounds. He counts the number of the stars; He gives names to all of them. Great is our Lord, and abundant in strength; His understanding is infinite." The Lord who counts the stars also counts the number of hairs on our head. Truly His understanding is infinite!

Are you giving comfort to a child who is wondering what life will be like tomorrow? Be encouraged because Christ

Himself was a child. Are you a teenager? Christ Himself was a teenager, understanding full well the temptations and challenges teenagers face. He lived in a police state, was slandered, lied about, and spat upon. And when you and I come to die, we can be assured that our Lord has already passed behind that curtain, making it safe for us to enter. He knows all things both actual and possible.

Jesus saw the coin in the depths of the sea, but He also sees the thoughts hidden in the depths of our hearts. All things are present to Him. Whatever your circumstance, *Jesus knows.*

Christ's Sovereign Kingship

When Peter was asked whether his Master paid the temple tax, he responded, "Yes." But notice carefully Christ's follow-up question: "From whom do the kings of the earth collect customs or poll-tax, from their sons or from strangers?"

The answer, of course, is that kings do not pay taxes. Taxes are paid only by the subjects of the kingdom. No king would think of levying a tax on his own family. No son would be obligated to pay a tax in his father's house.

Christ is under no obligation to pay a tax, because He is Lord of the earth and the universe. Why should He pay a temple tax if He is Lord of the temple? He owns all the shekels in the universe and much more besides. He owes not so much as a single drachma to any of His subjects.

Let us never forget God's ownership of the world, and more particularly, His ownership of us. We belong to God by virtue of creation, but we also belong to Him because of redemption. "Or do you not know that your body is a temple of the Holy Spirit who is in you, whom you have from God, and that you are not your own? For you have been bought with a price: therefore glorify God in your body" (1 Cor. 6:19-20).

God owns us and all of the possessions we so jealously guard for ourselves. To acknowledge God's ownership is to give up our petty insistence that we are owners of what He has given to us. We must take the title deeds and transfer them to His sovereign hands.

Why then did Christ pay the tax? He said He would pay the tax so that He would not give "offense." The Greek word is *skandalon,* and may be translated "stumbling block." Though Christ would not have had to pay the tax, He did it so that He would not be needlessly giving anyone an excuse to criticize Him. He wanted Peter and the disciples to learn that we should pay our share of taxes; we should do all we can to discharge our duty to even the questionable worship of the temple.

Though He owns all and owes nothing, Jesus gives that we might see His grace.

Christ's Sovereign Power

In the Creation account God gave man dominion over the beasts of the field, the fowls of the air, and the fish of the sea. We see His authority over the beasts of the field when He rode down the Mount of Olives on an unbroken colt. That animal was controlled by the One who rode on its back.

Christ also controlled the birds of the air and the roosters perched on hilltops. The night of Peter's betrayal all of the roosters were kept silent until Peter had denied the Lord three times, and then one rooster was allowed to cry out. There are many stories that illustrate Christ's control of the fish. We already noted that He performed a miracle when He asked Peter to "launch out into the deep for a catch." In John 21 there was a similar miracle when 153 fish were caught at Christ's command.

Here again Christ shows that He is Lord of the common experiences of life. Notice how the Master controlled three events that had to coincide for this miracle to occur.

First, *He directed someone to lose a coin,* a stater (or shekel), the exact amount that He and Peter would need to pay their tax. We don't know who lost it. Was it a child? Did the coin fall over the side of a boat? Did it slip through someone's pocket along the shore? However it got there, it was under the divine control of the Lord who intended to use it for His own purposes. In this case someone's loss would be Peter's gain.

Second, *He directed the fish to the coin.* To the fish this glittering object looked like a delicious dinner. We don't know whether this creature of the sea grasped for the coin as the object was sinking in the water or whether the coin was already resting on the bottom of the lake. Regardless, as the fish reached for its expected morsel, the object stuck in its mouth. That fish did not know that it carried its cargo for Christ.

Then third, *the Lord directed the fish to Peter's hook.* Though the sea was filled with thousands of fish, the text says that Peter was to open the mouth of the *first* fish he would catch, and it would have the prized possession. The timing of this event brought together various contingencies all directed by a precision that only the King of kings and Lord of lords was capable of.

Imagine Peter going to the Sea of Galilee and casting his hook. Perhaps young boys surrounded him and asked him questions. And Peter explained, "Just watch! The first fish I catch will have a shekel in its mouth!" And the boys were disbelieving until the fish was caught, Peter opened its mouth—and there was the promised coin!

Whenever Peter fished in obedience to Christ, he always caught something. He came to the same lake as before, used the same equipment, and had the same hopes . . . but everything had changed. Even fishing had a different meaning if it was done for Christ. All of nature responds to the "divine impulse."

Finally, *Christ is also sovereign over His followers.* He told Peter what to do and expected obedience. If He is King, we are servants; if He is our Master, we are His disciples. And if we should speak on His behalf (as Peter did to the tax collector), we had better know His mind. Since He is no longer physically present on earth, we can properly represent Him only when we spend time poring over His words in the New Testament. "If you abide in My word, then you are truly disciples of Mine" (John 8:31).

Christ is not a cold despot who rules us with an iron fist. Far from it. He told His disciples, "You are My friends, if you do what I command you. No longer do I call you slaves; for the slave does not know what his master is doing; but I have called you friends, for all things that I have heard from My Father I have made known to you" (15:14-15). This friendship results in partnership.

Read again Christ's words to Peter: "Take the coin and give it to them for you and Me." There were not two fish that needed to be caught, one for Peter and another for Christ. This *one* fish bearing *one* coin symbolized the partnership between Christ and Peter in meeting their obligations. If Peter were to give himself wholly to God, he would not be abandoned.

At least three people benefited from this miracle. First, the tax collector was satisfied. The work of the temple was helped and the sacrifices, such as they were, would be encouraged to continue.

Second, Christ benefited. He said to Peter the coin was "For you and Me." He is glorified by the special provisions He makes for His people. When He is not involved in supplying our needs, He loses glory.

To paraphrase F.B. Meyer, we see Christ in the wilderness

fighting Satan, surviving a forty-day fast; and we can hear Him say, "This is for you and Me." We follow Him to Gethsemane and to the cross where He writhed in pain and we hear Him say, "This is for you and Me." We see Him rising from the grave, and then ascending into heaven and we hear Him say, "This is for you and Me." And some day we will reign with Him forever, and we will hear Him say, "This is for you and Me." Though He is the Son of God, He is our Partner, our Brother.

Finally, Peter benefited. God delighted to stretch Peter's faith and to purify his worship and love. This was another gracious touch in the shaping of a man of God. Peter had to learn, as all of us do, that the greatest need we have is not financial, it is not relational, it is not even good health. Our greatest need is for faith, the ability to trust Christ to meet every one of our needs. Our greatest need is to understand the unique partnership we have with Him as our Lord and our Brother, taking care of us every step of the way.

Years later, Peter would understand this much better and write, "Humble yourselves, therefore, under the mighty hand of God, that He may exalt you at the proper time, casting all your anxiety upon Him, because He cares for you" (1 Peter 5:6-7).

The Christ who timed the miracle of the tribute money is the same One who directs our steps today. All we need to do is live with an attitude of surrender and faith and we will find that our partnership with Him is strong enough to help us weather the setbacks of life.

When Peter left his fishing business and became a partner in Christ's fishing industry, he had no idea that he would see such a display of divine power. Not only would he be able to share the Master's heart, but even the Master's coin.

And someday when we see Jesus, we all shall hear Him say, "This was for you and Me."

Chapter Eight

THE MASTER'S HUMBLE TOUCH

(Read John 13:1-20)

The world is a dirty place, spiritually speaking. The movies on television, the dishonesty prevalent in business, and general disregard for moral values — these influences have pressured many believers to compromise their convictions. The temptations confronting the younger generation are unparalleled in history.

But the real enemy is not without, it is within. We are born with a nature that quite naturally gravitates toward fleshly interests. The tainted desires within are only too receptive to the stimuli without. And even those of us committed to a life of purity find that every inch of progress is contested.

How can we be clean?

Back in 1986 an arsonist broke into the Moody Church in Chicago. He stole some things from my office, then decided to set the organ, piano, pulpit, and several oak chairs on fire.

Smoke damage throughout the church was extensive. Cleaning the building took thousands of man-hours. No matter how often we cleaned the seats in the auditorium, or the books and desks in our offices, we could still find soot hiding in the crevice of a chair or in a desk drawer.

Incredibly, the actions of one man (which probably took

10 minutes) caused grime to settle on 4,000 seats in the auditorium, the hymnals, the halls, and the Sunday School classrooms, not to mention the offices of the church. Though the arsonist was arrested and spent some time in jail, the consequences of his crime were not thereby diminished.

Just so Adam and Eve, by one act of disobedience, caused the smudge of sin to fall on every human heart. And throughout the centuries, man has tried to get himself clean. Try as we might, we cannot erase the stains. The soot of sin has settled in the human spirit, a place that cannot be reached by popular detergents.

One of the most common sins that needs to be uprooted from our hearts is pride, the subtle attitude that makes us think we are better than others. Pride makes us haphazard in our prayer life because we think we need God only in emergencies. And even after we accept Christ as Savior, pride can keep us from being a true servant.

Late one afternoon the disciples were wrangling over this question: Who is the greatest in the kingdom of heaven? They were expecting Christ to establish the kingdom, so they wondered, who might the prime minister be. And who would serve as secretary of state. That very evening Christ was scheduled to eat the Last Supper with them. In that environment, He gave them a powerful lesson about humility and spiritual cleansing.

As we might expect, Peter was involved in the much-needed discourse. Christ used his reactions and questions to teach some lessons all of us need to learn. Once again the Master Sculptor chiseled a bit more of those fleshly attitudes from Peter's character. He also proved His ability to cleanse Peter from every taint of impurity lurking in the heart and conscience.

In those days people wore open sandals or thongs, and their feet became dusty as they walked along the dirt paths.

Servants were expected to wash the feet of guests to make them feel both welcome and comfortable. Jesus had asked the disciples to prepare the Upper Room so that He might be able to eat the Passover meal with them. When the thirteen men arrived, no servant was available. As the disciples looked at one another, wondering who would stoop to wash their feet, Jesus surprised them: "[Jesus] rose from supper, and laid aside His garments; and taking a towel, girded Himself about. Then He poured water into the basin, and began to wash the disciples' feet, and to wipe them with the towel with which He was girded" (John 13:4-5).

Let's consider the three lessons Christ taught Peter and the other disciples. Lessons we all must learn.

The Lesson on Servanthood

The disciples must have been shocked and embarrassed. The Son of God was girded with a towel, and now He was bending down, washing the feet of one disciple and then another! How could He stoop so low! The Creator was washing the feet of the creature! Incredibly, *God was on His hands and knees.*

Indeed, these hands created the worlds and spoke them into existence; now these hands were to wash dirty feet. Christ obviously was secure, living with the full knowledge that He did not have to maintain the decorum expected of a king. He could humble Himself because the expectations of others were unimportant. His source of strength came from inner self-assurance and a steady peace that controlled his every move.

The key phrase in this story is in verse 3: "Jesus knowing." Christ's confidence was so deeply rooted that He could take the lowly position without having His dignity threatened. What, specifically, did He know that made Him believe that washing dirty feet was not beneath His dignity?

First, *He knew His mission.* "His hour had come that He should depart out of this world to the Father, having loved His own who were in the world, He loved them to the end" (v. 1). This was the hour into which would be compressed the darkness of Gethsemane and the horror of the cross. Yet this was precisely the reason why Christ had come into the world—the will of God was being done.

Second, *He knew His resources.* "Knowing that the Father had given all things into His hands" (v. 3). Yes, even the subtle plans of Judas, made under the instigation of Satan, were fully under Christ's control. This gave Him the confidence that His own future would not be left to chance but to the certainty of God's will.

Third, *He knew His origin.* "Knowing . . . that He had come forth from God" (v. 3). He remembered the glories of heaven, the fellowship with the Father, and the plan that He would come to redeem a part of the human race. He was secure in His heavenly mission.

Finally, *He knew His destination.* He was returning to the Father (v. 3). Between the point of His earthly origin and the point of His destination there lay the agony of Gethsemane and the horror of the cross. Yet because He knew how it would all end, He could face this trial with confidence: "who for the joy set before Him endured the cross, despising the shame, and has sat down at the right hand of the throne of God" (Heb. 12:2).

With such a sense of mission, Christ was able to take a lowly place in the midst of His disciples. What He did was not as important to Him as the One for whom He did it. Even an ordinary task becomes extraordinary if it is done with the right motive.

Today, many people seek a job they love, and it is delightful when they find one. But millions of others will never find a vocation they love, and yet they can find fulfillment. Paul taught that even slaves could have the honor of working for God rather than men, if they see their lot from God's perspective (Eph. 6:5-8). We can try to find a vocation that is in keeping with our training, aptitude, and dignity. Sometimes applicants are rejected because they have too much education or too much experience. It is difficult to be satisfied with a lesser responsibility.

Never has one been so overqualified as Christ the Son of God, washing His disciples' feet! He who was higher than the heavens stepped down lower than a housemaid. Little wonder He often used a small child to teach the meaning of true greatness.

The Lesson on Submission

"And so He came to Simon Peter. He said to Him, 'Lord, do You wash my feet?' Jesus answered and said to him, 'What I do you do not realize now; but you shall understand hereafter.' Peter said to Him, 'Never shall You wash my feet!' Jesus answered him, 'If I do not wash you, you have no part with Me' " (John 13:6-7).

A superficial reading of this exchange might lead us to conclude that Peter's statement reflected humility. The opposite, however, is likely the case. Subtly, imperceptibly, his unwillingness to let Christ wash his feet was a form of pride.

First of all, Peter felt uncomfortable because he knew that Christ was doing what he (Peter) should have done. It is not easy to have someone wash your feet, especially someone who is above you in the authority structure. There are some Christians who believe that the washing of feet is an ordinance in the church, and they practice it several times a year. Men wash the feet of men; women wash the feet of women. But what do they do before they attend church that evening? You guessed it, they all wash their own feet! By nature, we do not want someone to wash our feet, and here was the

God of the universe stooping to do just that. Peter was embarrassed because receiving a gift of service reminds us of our own need. In the process our pride is wounded.

Second, Peter was actually displaying pride by disagreeing with Christ! After all, if the Son of God wished to wash his feet, who was he to say otherwise? The Gospels record three times that Peter disagreed with his Master. We recall when Christ explained that He was going to the cross, Peter rebuked Him: "This shall never happen to You." As we noted in that instance, if Christ had taken his advice, Peter himself would have been lost forever.

Peter also disagreed here, insisting that Christ would not wash his feet. And later that same evening, Peter drew his sword and cut off the ear of the servant of the high priest. (He probably intended to kill the man but missed.) Christ responded, "Put the sword into the sheath; the cup which the Father has given Me, shall I not drink it?" (John 18:11)

Though it appears as humility, it is really pride that makes us uncomfortable in receiving Christ's gifts. It is also pride that says, "I've sinned too much for God to forgive me." Though God says Christ's death was a complete sacrifice for sin, we think that we know better. Under the guise of humility, some people believe they have found a sin that could not be covered by the work of the cross. Do we really know better than God?

Christ responded to Peter, "If I wash thee not, thou hast no part with Me" (13:8, KJV). There is more to this story than meets the eye. Christ is not just thinking about washing Peter's feet, but about the spiritual washing that is so necessary for every one of us.

Peter, thinking only of physical washing, responds, "Lord, not my feet only, but also my hands and my head!" (v. 9) If a little washing is good, much washing is better!

Peter may not always have thought deeply, but he always

felt deeply. His love for Christ was single-minded, clear, and public.

A Lesson on Cleansing

Peter had misunderstood the symbolism. He had already had a bath; he didn't need another one. Only his feet were dirty. So Christ explained, *"He who has bathed needs only to wash his feet, but is completely clean; and you are clean, but not all of you"* (v. 10).

With that Jesus washed Peter's feet, then sat down to give a further explanation of what He had just done. This act not only got their feet clean, it was to serve as an illustration of spiritual cleansing and an example of humble service.

Clean feet are a picture of a clean heart. The dust of the streets is symbolic of the smudge of this world. Christ is teaching what it means to be cleansed, and also the need to distinguish between a "bath" and having one's feet washed. There are two washings signified by two Greek words in this passage. There is a bath (*luow*), which is the bath of regeneration, or justification. It is the complete cleansing that takes place when we accept Christ as our Savior and become one of His. God declares us to be as righteous as Christ Himself is! This bath cleanses us forever and we need it only once. This washing takes away our sins—past, present, and future—since He has "canceled out the certificate of debt consisting of decrees against us and which was hostile to us; and He has taken it out of the way, having nailed it to the cross" (Col. 2:14).

New Christians often ask, "After I'm saved and I sin, do I have to be saved again?" The answer is no! The bath of regeneration never loses its power. Once we accept Christ as our Savior, we are sealed by the Holy Spirit until the day of redemption (Eph. 4:30); we are adopted into God's family (Rom. 8:15); joined to Christ as a member of His body

(Eph. 5:30); and our names have been *"written from the foundation of the world in the Book of Life of the Lamb who has been slain"* (Rev. 13:8). God is not about to undo what He has so securely done. He does not leave His children for adoption, or lose them in a child custody battle.

There is a second bath (*nipto*), the washing of the feet. This cleansing takes place repeatedly, every day when we admit our sins to God. It is the washing of 1 John 1:9: "If we confess our sins, He is faithful and righteous to forgive us our sins and to cleanse us from all unrighteousness." You can measure your own spiritual maturity by asking how long it takes you to get back into fellowship after becoming aware of sin. Carnal Christians let their sins stack up; those who walk in the Spirit confess their sins at the very moment they become aware of them. This is sometimes called "keeping current accounts with God."

Peter learned that this washing demands submission. It means that we let Christ wash us even though we may be embarrassed for committing the same sin again and again. Often those who get caught in a cycle of failure do so simply because their submission to Christ is incomplete. Confession means that we agree fully with God, even giving up our right to commit that sin again. The goal of confession is to restore our fellowship with God and to give us a basis for spiritual victory and freedom.

What did Christ mean when He said to Peter, "If I do not wash you, you have no part with Me"? (John 13:8) As a believer, Peter was already joined to his Master, and after the Ascension he would be a member of Christ's body. When Christ said that washing was necessary in order to have a part with Him, He was referring to personal fellowship. This is the meaning of the word *part* in Luke 10:42, where Christ commends Mary for having chosen "the good part, which shall not be taken away from her." And in 2 Corinthians

6:15, Paul says that Christians have no "part" (KJV) with demons. That means we have no fellowship with them.

Within a few hours, Peter would deny Christ. He would grieve because of his weakness and fear of claiming Christ as a friend. Spiritually speaking, he would become dirty again, and would have to have his feet washed. He would have to humbly accept the washing of Christ. But he would not have to experience the *bath of regeneration* again.

Christ invites us to His table, but we must have clean feet and hands. "Behold, I stand at the door and knock; if any one hears My voice and opens the door, I will come in to him, and will dine with him, and he with Me" (Rev. 3:20). To come with the mud and the impurity of the world is to cut ourselves off from the sweetness of His love and the intimacy He so fervently desires.

The closer we come to Calvary, the more dirt we will see on our feet. Even the smallest specks of mud become visible while standing in the presence of Christ. Even the most insignificant sin will become a millstone around our necks. "A little leaven leavens the whole lump" (1 Cor. 5:6). Tozer said, "That part of us which we try to rescue from the cross becomes the seat of our troubles."

One man among the circle of disciples did not have his feet washed (figuratively, not literally). Jesus said to Peter, "You are clean, but not all of you" (John 13:10). John, who was recording this story, adds, "For He knew the one who was betraying Him; for this reason He said, 'Not all of you are clean' " (v. 11).

Peter needed his feet washed; Judas had never had a bath! This apostate was apparently able to do the same miracles as other disciples, and was such a crafty hypocrite that he did not attract special notice. When Christ said to the group, "Truly, truly, I say to you, that one of you will betray Me" (v. 21), to their everlasting credit they did not suspect Judas but asked, "Is it I?" (Matt. 26:21-22, KJV)

Just imagine: Judas was with Jesus for three years, playing the religious game so well that the disciples did not suspect that he was the one who would betray their Lord. He walked the walk and talked the talk with incredible hypocrisy. But in the end, he was unwashed and lost forever. Though Christ had washed Judas' feet, Christ had never washed his heart. And even today, there are many whom we believe to be Christians, but who someday will be revealed as frauds, wholly filled with the fruit of hypocrisy. Christ said of Judas, "It would have been good for that man if he had not been born" (v. 24).

What is the bottom line? *If you have not been washed by Christ, you are dirty, no matter how pleasant you appear to be on the outside.* The humility that caused Christ to stoop from the glories of heaven to the dirt of a washbasin is the same humility we must have to enter the kingdom of heaven. Only He can speak us clean; He can give us the bath that leads to heaven, and He can keep us cleansed as we walk through this dirty world.

Peter learned that humility is an attribute of a man of God. It makes a rough stone smooth, and a sinner a little bit more like Christ.

Will you let Him wash you?

Chapter Nine

FROM REGRET
TO RESTORATION

(Read Luke 22:31-62)

"For of all the sad words of tongue and pen, the saddest are
these, 'It might have been.'" So wrote John Greenleaf Whit-
tier.

All of us can identify with that statement. We know how
painful regret can be. To have missed an opportunity or to
have made a painful mistake can lead us to the brink of
despair. We keep thinking how really different it all could
have been, if . . . if . . . if. . . . You complete the sentence.

There are two kinds of regret. There is the regret caused by
human error. A missionary airplane mechanic had an excellent record in servicing airplanes. One day he had just com-
pleted the initial hand-tightening on a nut when he was
called away. Completely distracted by the new problem, he
forgot to tighten the nut with a wrench. The airplane took
off with seven people in it. The loose nut let gasoline leak out
of the motor. The plane eventually caught fire and crashed,
killing all seven aboard.

At the funeral the mechanic saw the seven coffins lined up
in a row. Waves of regret washed over him in agony of soul
and spirit. One momentary lapse and seven lives had been
snuffed out. Here were seven new widows, many of them
with children who had lost their fathers. Put yourself in the

mechanic's shoes and feel, as far as possible, the deep regret he experienced.

You may have been driving carefully in a residential district. The curb was lined with cars. You were momentarily distracted by a person on one side of the street. As your eyes refocused on the road ahead of you, you saw a toddler run into the street. You slammed on the brakes, but it was too late. By the time the ambulance arrived you already suspected the worst.

About all that we can do in such situations is ask others to forgive us for our errors in judgment. Hopefully, the mother of the child will understand despite her deep grief. The missionary mechanic was fortunate because he was assured by the bereaved widows that they would not be angry at him for making a mistake. Receiving the forgiveness of others enabled him to forgive himself.

Such feelings of regret are not the promptings of the Holy Spirit. We are all prone to human error. An honest mistake is very different from willful sin, though the consequences might be similar. God does not want us to be overcome with regret; for even such mistakes fall within the circle of His divine providence. We must forgive ourselves. Our mistakes must be put behind us.

A second form of regret grows out of deliberate disobedience. We choose a certain lifestyle even though we know it is wrong. A small voice tells us our choice is sinful, but we continue to follow our willful desires. One day we page through the family album and see a picture of ourselves and suddenly we wonder what life would have been like if our choices had been different.

Or the regret may come at the end of life, as death approaches. A friend went to see a former employer, a newspaper publisher, in the hospital. "I know I am going to die," he began. "I have wasted my life in a vain pursuit of riches and public acclaim. Now I realize my mistake and want to get right with God." Better late than never, but oh, the pain of regret!

Peter felt both the pain and the blessing of regret. Interestingly, the one disciple who loved Christ so fervently is the very one who denied Him so vehemently.

Read Luke 22:31-34 carefully, for it sets the stage for a denial that Peter, the disciple of Christ, will deeply bemoan. God will use it to teach him about grace and to help him make the best of his future. And we will learn from his mistake.

Jesus concluded the Last Supper with a promise that the disciples would eventually sit at His table in the kingdom, and judge the twelve tribes of Israel. But then He turned to Peter for a special, personal word: "Simon, Simon, behold, Satan has demanded permission to sift you like wheat; but I have prayed for you, that your faith may not fail; and you, when once you have turned again, strengthen your brothers" (Luke 22:31-32).

If Peter was going to be restored, obviously the implication is that he was about to fall. This news was not well-received, particularly by someone whose commitment to Christ was fervent, single-minded, and unquestioned. He had all the credentials for being a winning member of the team, so he decided to reassure Jesus. "Lord, with You I am ready to go both to prison and to death!" (v. 33)

Jesus was not impressed. Have you ever thought that God had a right to be proud of your commitment and promise of obedience? We can keep no promises except those made in total dependence, recognizing our own frailty. The usual pattern is, the bigger the promise, the bigger the fall.

You know the rest of the story. Peter obviously *boasted too much; prayed too little* (he fell asleep in Gethsemane); *acted too soon* (he cut off the ear of the servant of the high priest);

followed too far (from a distance); and *thought too late* (he remembered the prediction of Christ only when the rooster crowed).

We read, "And the Lord turned and looked at Peter. And Peter remembered the word of the Lord, how He had told him, 'Before a cock crows today, you will deny Me three times' " (v. 61).

Why did Peter weep bitterly? (v. 62) He was in the very presence of Jesus when he denied Him. Jesus was within the line of his vision when the servant girl came and said to him, "This man was with Him too" (v. 56). There in the presence of the One he loved, he denied it, saying, "Woman, I do not know Him" (v. 56).

And if such a denial is shocking to us, let us remember that he denied it a *second* time! And when some bystanders were saying that they saw him with Christ, he began to curse and swear, "I do not know this fellow you are talking about!" (Mark 14:71) *Three* times! He swore he did not know his Lord!

Peter had been with Jesus three years. He had shared the platform with Him at many large gatherings. Jesus had healed his mother-in-law. And Peter had made that soul-stirring affirmation, "Thou art the Christ, the Son of the living God" (Matt. 16:16). Now the accusing tone in a girl's voice brought from Peter's lips a refusal to admit that he knew his Savior. There was something about the look of Christ that tore at Peter's heart. Think of the shame and regret!

How did Christ bring Peter back into fellowship? What were the dynamics of this encounter? Thankfully, God draws back the curtain and lets us see what really happened on earth and in heaven. In the process we are shown how we can come back to Christ, no matter how deep our guilt and regret may be. Four truths should encourage us.

Christ Intercedes for Us

Knowing what was about to happen, Christ prayed for Peter. He addressed His disciple as Simon, for this night the rock would revert back to sand. "Simon, Simon, behold, Satan has demanded permission to sift you like wheat; but I have prayed for you, that your faith may not fail; and you, when once you have turned again, strengthen your brothers" (v. 31).

Christ prayed for Peter specifically. This is clear in the Greek New Testament when Jesus said, "Satan has demanded permission to sift you," the Greek word *you* is plural. Satan had demanded permission to sift all of the disciples. But when He continued, "but I have prayed for you," that word *you* is singular. The focus of Christ's prayer was Peter. He was the one who needed the special strength at the moment.

Why did Jesus pray for Peter? Was it because Peter held such a lofty position in the group? Hardly. Peter was the rash and egotistical one. He was not the mild-mannered, consistent follower. Was it because Peter was bold and able to make wise decisions?

Wrong again. The reason Jesus prayed for Peter was precisely because he was so weak, so easily tripped up in his spiritual perception. Show me a man who is wretched, who is broken up emotionally, who cries out to God in the agony of his soul; you show me a woman who is fallen and crushed by her sin, who is unstable and unable to get a grip on her emotions, and I will show you a person upon whom the grace and mercy of Jesus Christ rests.

You remember the story of the shepherd. He had ninety-nine fine, obedient sheep in the fold. Yet there was one that had gone astray, who was out in the night, and that is the one the shepherd pursued (Luke 15:4-6). Jesus sees everyone reading this page, but He is particularly looking at the one who is following afar off, the one whose faith has almost failed, and the one who feels outside of the embrace of God. He has prayed for you personally, as He prayed for Peter.

Significantly, Jesus' prayer is not a "bless everyone" generalization. He prays against Satan's coming assault. He prays that the devil's victory will be turned to defeat. When wheat grows, a coating called chaff protects the grain. In the old-fashioned winnowing of Jesus' day, the chaff was separated from the wheat by walking an animal on the husks and throwing the mixture into the air so that the wind could blow the chaff away. Modern harvesting equipment uses a sieve. Jesus was saying to Peter, "Satan wants to sift you and prove that you are nothing but chaff."

Does our exposure to temptation have anything to do with evil spirits? Yes. Peter may not have realized that his fear originated with the devil. But the Lord opened the veil so that we can glimpse behind the scenes and know that there was more to this battle than meets the eye. In the spirit world a vicious battle was in progress for Peter's heart.

Thirty years later Peter would write, "Be of sober spirit, be on the alert. Your adversary, the devil, prowls about like a roaring lion, seeking someone to devour. But resist him, firm in your faith, knowing that the same experiences of suffering are being accomplished by your brethren who are in the world" (1 Peter 5:8-9). The devil seeks to destroy our witness for Christ. In the unseen world there is constant conflict; there is a battle in which we are involved.

In temptation four personalities are involved: Satan, Christ, angels, and of course we find ourselves in the middle of the conflict. Lewis Sperry Chafer, the founder of Dallas Seminary, used to say, "A secret sin on earth is an open scandal in heaven." Satan accuses us; Christ prays for us; the angels observe God's love and justice exercised on our behalf. *What we think is classified information on earth is in the public domain in heaven.*

Every Christian goes through this sifting process. For some it may be illness, the loss of a job, or a failed relationship. But for many it is temptation, the constant inner struggles of the soul where our allegiance to Christ is tested. Satan not only has tempted us, but likely has made meticulous plans for our downfall. Like a snake, he is coiled, waiting to strike at an appropriate time. He magnifies the power of temptation, trying to get us to follow the easy path; he wants our lives to discredit Christ.

We can imagine Christ saying to us as He did to Peter, "Satan has asked permission, and it has been granted, that you might be tested. When the temptation is over, I pray that your faith will not fail. And when you have turned back, strengthen your brethren. Learn from your failures and keep going."

We have a faithful friend who represents us in heaven. Christ is our High Priest who stands in our stead before God the Father, "For we do not have a high priest who cannot sympathize with our weaknesses, but one who has been tempted in all things as we are, yet without sin" (Heb. 4:15). Christ not only died for us, today He lives for us. He is on our side in the struggle, fully aware of Satan's strength and strategy. And, of course, He is able to pick us up if we fall.

Christ Understands Us

Remember Jesus said to Peter, "The cock will not crow today until you have denied three times that you know Me" (Luke 22:34). Did He predict Peter's failure simply to prove His omniscience? No, Christ never used His divine attributes to impress anyone; He used His power and knowledge for the benefit of His people. He was making it easy for Peter to return to fellowship after his impending fall. Jesus wanted Peter to remember that He knew in advance both the circumstances he would be in and the fear that would cause him to stumble. *Grace was announced before Peter fell.* Christ trusted Peter with His heart of love.

Christ knew where Peter would be seated; He knew that a servant girl would walk by and accuse Peter of belonging to Jesus. The Savior knew there would be a rooster in the area who would be restrained until the right time to alert Peter of his sin. The Bible report reveals that while Peter was *still speaking,* the rooster began crowing—perfect timing.

A student came to me one day and said, "I can't face God about this same sin again. I can't come into God's presence with my guilt and shame." She thought that God might not be able to handle the disappointment. But our Lord is never caught off guard. He knows our weakness and the full extent of our propensity to sin. Jesus knows things about us that we have not even admitted to ourselves. When Jeremiah said that, "The heart is more deceitful than all else, and is desperately sick; who can understand it?" he followed it with the words, "*I,* the Lord, search the heart, *I* test the mind" (Jer. 17:9-10, italics added). Unlike an earthly father, Christ will never say to us, "*I* never expected that you would do such a thing!"

We could never stand for a moment without the glories of grace. Our fall is known to a Savior who will restore us to fellowship and give us another assignment. "For a righteous man falls seven times, and rises again, but the wicked stumble in time of calamity" (Prov. 24:16). Thankfully, the well of grace will never run dry.

Christ Has Compassion for Us

Christ prays for us. He knows our circumstances and weaknesses and shows us compassion. He sees our hurt, anger, and shame. He sees the love that we have for Him and the regret our sin has caused us. And He cares.

If you have experienced deep regret, you will have some

idea of the torture Peter must have gone through for three long days. He had promised that he would stand with Christ until death, and now he buckled under a bit of pressure. Imagine what he felt after news of his Master's crucifixion reached him. "My last chance to prove my loyalty! *I denied Him, not once, not twice, but three times! As long as I live I will never be able to change the past.... I can't forgive myself!*" His own oaths rang in his ears.

If someone now had asked Peter, "Are you a disciple of Jesus?" he may very well have said, "I was one, but I am no longer worthy of that high honor. I'm no longer one of the twelve disciples. The book on me is closed." Might it not be that Peter thought he was the one about whom Christ spoke at the Last Supper, "One of you shall betray Me"? Perhaps the traitor was not Judas after all but Peter, the one who promised allegiance to his Master!

After Christ was dead, He was put into a new tomb in a nearby garden. Some women came to the tomb on the first day of the week to anoint the body. They were wondering who would roll the heavy stone from the entrance when, to their surprise, they noticed that it had already been pushed aside.

When they entered, they saw a young man sitting at the right wearing a white robe. Incredibly, he told them that Jesus was no longer there, for He was risen! Then the angel added, "But go, tell His disciples and Peter" (Mark 16:7). *And Peter!*

Why does Peter receive honorable mention? Christ knew that if he were not specifically mentioned by name he would never feel worthy of being included among the disciples. This was Christ's overture; it was the Master's hand extended to a fallen comrade.

Even more grace followed. Luke tells a story of two disciples walking en route to Emmaus when they were unknowingly joined by Jesus. After Christ revealed Himself to them, they returned to Jerusalem that same evening where they were greeted with the news, "The Lord has really risen, and has appeared to Simon" (Luke 24:34).

He appeared to Simon!

In 1 Corinthians 15 the Apostle Paul listed those to whom Christ had appeared after His resurrection. Interestingly, Peter (Cephas) appears at the top of the list. This confirms that Peter was the first to see Jesus after the Resurrection. Peter did not have to feel like an outcast any longer. A compassionate Jesus had forgiven him.

By His actions, Christ was saying, "Peter, you fell, but you are not down. You were ashamed to say you knew Me, but I am glad to say that I know you. You have sinned, but you have wept tears of repentance and you are forgiven. I love you, Peter."

Even now the arms of Jesus are reaching out to us, no matter our failures. Those arms are long and gentle enough to embrace even the most wayward, backslidden person who has denied the Savior. Jesus has His eyes fastened on us, saying, "I have compassion on you. I assure you that you can come back into fellowship with the living God."

Christ Restores Us

Haddon Robinson tells the story of a man named Roy Riggles, who caught a football and ran sixty-five yards in the wrong direction while playing in a Rose Bowl game for UCLA. One of his teammates outdistanced him and tackled him just before he scored for Georgia Tech, the opposing team.

Since that play came in the first half, the crowd wondered what coach Nibbs Price would do with Roy Riggles in the second half. In humiliation Riggles put a blanket around his shoulders, sat down in a corner, put his face in his hands and cried like a baby. When it was time to return to the field, the coach said simply, "The same team that played the first half will play the second half."

Riggles didn't budge. The coach repeated his instructions but the weeping player said, "I can't do it; I have humiliated you. I've ruined the University of California; I've ruined myself; I couldn't face that crowd in the stadium."

Then Coach Nibbs Price put his hands on Riggles' shoulders and said, "Roy, get up and go back. The game is only half over." And when Roy Riggles went back, the Georgia Tech players will tell you that they have never seen a man play football as Roy Riggles played in that second half.

In one of the most tender scenes in the Bible, Jesus lets Peter know that the game is not yet over. Peter had gone back to fishing, evidently thinking that his work for Christ was over. But Jesus met him along the shore of Galilee just as He had three years before. Once again He gave the instructions, "Cast the net on the right-hand side of the boat, and you will find a catch" (John 21:6). They obeyed and caught 153 fish!

Incredibly, after they came to shore they noticed that Jesus *already* had breakfast prepared for them! We do not know where the bread and the fish came from, but why should we speculate, since we are speaking of Christ, the Lord. Over breakfast the Lord had a few words with Peter.

" 'Simon, son of John, do you love Me more than these?' He said to Him, 'Yes, Lord, You know that I love You.' He said to him, 'Tend My lambs' " (v. 15). Christ used the Greek word *agape,* which refers to the highest form of love. Peter responded with *phileo,* a reference to brotherly love. Christ may have picked up on the change of words and hence replied, "Feed My lambs," a hint that Peter may not yet be ready for his fuller ministry.

Jesus then repeated the question, again asking if Peter had

that true *agape* love for Him. Peter, not yet sure of his own heart, responded, "Yes, Lord, You know that I love [*phileo*] You." Jesus replied, "Shepherd My sheep" (v. 16). Yes, Jesus had confidence that Peter could do even more than just feed the lambs.

A third time Jesus asked the same question, but this time He used the word for *love* which Peter had used: "Simon, son of John, do you love [*phileo*] Me?" Peter was disturbed that his commitment of brotherly love was not enough, so he repeated his affirmation of love, this time using the stronger word, *agape*.

"Lord, You know all things; You know that I love You." Jesus accepted this and replied, "Tend My sheep" (v. 17). No matter how unsure Peter may have been of himself, Christ wanted him to know that he had been fully restored. He was called to the high honor of shepherding the Lord's sheep.

Three times Peter had denied Christ; three times he was given the privilege of affirming his love for Him. The dark days of humiliation were over. Regret was replaced by responsibility, partnership, and full acceptance. Christ's prayer was answered. Peter would now restore his brothers.

Christ's prayer did not keep Peter from falling. His prayer did, however, result in Peter's restoration. Peter was brought back from the abyss and now he was able to strengthen his brothers. The Lord's sheep would be fed, the rock would remain steadfast.

Sometimes those who have fallen the furthest are the most effective in strengthening the feet of those who have slipped. Peter's knowledge of his own heart enabled him to preach effectively; and his own weaknesses made him write 1 and 2 Peter with sensitivity and insight. Millions have been made strong because of the lessons Peter learned in the school of failure.

The Sifting Process

Three people were sifted that night in Gethsemane. Christ was sifted and found to be grain. Perhaps Satan actually tried to kill Christ in those dark moments of torture. Despite the pain and temptation, Christ was indeed shown to be pure wheat.

Judas was also sifted the same evening. He kissed Jesus on the cheek as a show of friendship, yet was a partner in a plot to have the Master crucified. He was so filled with remorse that he went and hanged himself. He was proved to be pure chaff.

Peter was sifted and, like most of us, was shown to be part chaff and part wheat. This process of sifting was one of God's ways of separating the chaff from the wheat. As Peter saw his helplessness and learned to depend on the Holy Spirit, much of the chaff was blown away.

Outwardly, Peter and Judas did a similar deed—both denied Christ. Judas, instead of repenting, let the regret and remorse overwhelm him. He refused the forgiveness that would have cleansed his polluted conscience. He took his regret with him into eternity.

Peter, on the other hand, responded to the look of the Savior. His regret and restoration made his love for Christ much stronger. Those who are forgiven much, love much.

While walking in a redwood forest in California, I noticed a tree that had fallen many years ago. A new tree was now growing straight toward heaven, using the fallen tree as a part of its root system. Though the fallen tree had long since lost its glory, it had become part of a new structure.

God uses our regrets and failures to make us stronger in our faith and witness. If we are willing to learn from our experience, our failures will not be wasted. It is never too late to come back.

Like Roy Riggles, we sometimes take the ball and run in

the wrong direction. We stumble and fall and are so filled with shame that we don't want to try again. And then the grace of God comes and says, "Get up . . . go back, the game is only half over." This is the Gospel of the second chance; the Gospel for those who have fallen once too often. The Gospel of the Loving Coach.

Christ is even now praying for us. He knows our weaknesses and the circumstances that caused us to fall. He is also filled with compassion, and is willing to restore us to fellowship and usefulness. We must simply let Him provide the healing that only He can give.

Peter had to learn that, even when we betray Christ, He does not betray us. Though we may be rough and twisted, the divine Sculptor will hew us according to His special plan. And when we are damaged, He repairs the hurt.

The game is not yet over. Join the Master for breakfast in Galilee.

(Parts of chap. 9 were adapted from Erwin Lutzer, *Managing Your Emotions*, Wheaton, Ill.: Victor Books, 1983, chap. 10.)

Chapter Ten

STRENGTHENED BY THE MASTER'S GRIP

(Read Acts 2:14-36; 3:11-26; 4:18-22)

Can human nature be changed? Or are the behavioral ruts too deep, the basic stuff of the human psyche too calcified? Are we stuck with our personality type no matter how negative, angry, or fearful we might be?

C.S. Lewis says, "It may be hard for an egg to turn into a bird; it would be a jolly sight harder for it to learn to fly while remaining an egg. We are like eggs at present. And you cannot go on indefinitely being just an ordinary, decent egg. We must be hatched or go bad" (*Mere Christianity* [New York, MacMillan, 1960], p. 169). Thankfully, God helps us get hatched!

Peter gives hope to those who think that change is impossible. Christ had promised him that he would become a rock, a stone in the foundation of the church. And, as we have learned, if the change would happen, Christ would be the One who would bring it about. First, Peter's heart would be changed by Christ's power. Then second, circumstances and the very presence of Christ would be the chisel that would mold Peter into the man Christ wanted him to be. We've already noticed changes in his life, but now the contrast becomes even more remarkable. With the coming of the Holy Spirit, Peter is indeed a new man.

From the beginning of their friendship, Peter had a single-minded devotion to Christ. But he was compulsive, vacillating, and at times a coward. *In the Gospels he is the cocoon; in the Book of Acts he becomes a butterfly.* Or to put it differently, the fertilized egg gets hatched.

Acts 2 is best known because it describes how the Holy Spirit came upon believers and they began to speak in tongues, that is, in the languages of those countries that bordered Israel. This special gift was given to the Jewish people as a sign that the era of the Gentiles had now come to pass. The Good News would no longer be limited to the beautiful Hebrew language but would be spoken in the diverse Gentile languages represented in Jerusalem. The gift of tongues was always actual languages; these languages could be interpreted by those who knew the particular tongue. Or, sometimes, God may have also given the interpreter the ability to understand a foreign language supernaturally. He was making a powerful statement that the Gospel would now go to all the nations of the world.

But more important than this special gift was the inner transformation that God brought about in the apostles by the filling of the Holy Spirit. The promised gift arrived with the sound of a rushing wind, and with it came an empowering that would make this small group of believers band together to shake the world.

Fifty days had elapsed since Christ's resurrection. During forty of those days Christ was with His disciples, preparing them for the great work that lay ahead. Then, at His ascension, He told the disciples to wait in Jerusalem for the promised Holy Spirit. After ten days in the Upper Room, the miracle happened. Though all the disciples were changed as a result of the Spirit's coming, Peter the spokesman is the clearest example of a transformation. He scarcely resembles the vacillating man we see in the Gospel accounts.

Let's consider the contrasts.

From Confusion to Understanding

A boy who was trying to put a puzzle together was driven to despair because the pieces simply did not seem to form a symmetrical picture. Only when he discovered that some pieces from another puzzle had been carelessly thrown onto the pile did he realize why he could not make sense of the picture he was trying to create.

In the Gospels Peter had some important pieces of the puzzle but the big picture didn't fit. He had disagreed with Christ, telling his Master that He should not let Himself be nailed to a cross. As I pointed out, Peter meant well but if Christ had taken his suggestion, Peter himself would not have been redeemed. Although he had the insight to recognize Christ as the Son of God, he simply did not understand the cross or the purpose of God in redemption.

Now Peter gives an eloquent sermon, explaining with penetrating insight the purpose of the cross and how it fits into God's eternal plan (Acts 2:14-36). This message which comprises twenty-two verses contains no less than twelve quotations from the Old Testament. Peter weaves together prophecy and divine providence. He ends his discourse with these words: "Men of Israel, listen to these words: Jesus the Nazarene, a Man attested to you by God with miracles and wonders and signs which God performed through Him in your midst, just as you yourselves know—this Man, delivered up by the predetermined plan and foreknowledge of God, you nailed to a cross by the hands of godless men and put Him to death" (vv. 22-23).

At last Peter put the cross in the center of God's program for Planet Earth. He now understood that the suffering of Christ was preordained as God's means of salvation. He proclaimed this publicly, no longer fearing the hostility of men though he knew they hated what he was saying. Let the whole world be against him; Christ was standing at his side.

Why this change in Peter's understanding? The Holy Spirit, Christ promised, would lead the disciples into truth because He was the Spirit of wisdom, and revelation. The Holy Spirit enlightens the mind; He helps us grasp the deeper meaning of Scripture and make sense out of God's relationship with the world. "Now we have received, not the spirit of the world, but the Spirit who is from God, that we might know the things freely given to us by God. . . . But a natural man does not accept the things of the Spirit of God; for they are foolishness to him, and he cannot understand them, because they are spiritually appraised" (1 Cor. 2:12, 14).

New Agers today also claim enlightenment, a form of revelation that initiates them into "hidden wisdom." Some have a mystical experience that propels them into another world. This, of course, is a satanic delusion. For one thing, such revelations are contrary to the Scriptures; for another, these experiences eventually lead to confusion, the exaltation of man, and satanic bondage. Let us take care to distinguish between the two opposing spirits in the world.

When God gives wisdom and revelation, it is always through a better understanding of the Scriptures and never independent of the divine Word. Satan is also a spirit of confusion, who gives thoughts that lead to frustration and uncertainty; God's revelation brings stability, direction, and wisdom.

Thanks to the Holy Spirit, Peter's *mind* was enlightened and the misunderstandings dissipated as he began to see more clearly God's purposes. Today the Holy Spirit, through the Word, does the same for us.

From Fear to Confidence

There is an Indian fable about a mouse that was in constant distress because of its fear of the cat. A magician took pity on the mouse and turned it into a cat, but then it became afraid of the dog. So the magician turned it into a dog and immediately it began to fear the tiger. Then, as a tiger, it began to fear the hunter! In the end the mouse was content to be a mouse again!

There is always something for us to fear. If it is not fear of poverty, it is fear of bad health, or fear of crime, or fear of death. The one answer for fear is *the conviction that God will be with us, no matter what.*

Remember that Peter, in response to the question of the servant girl, denied that he even knew Christ. In fact he swore, adamantly insisting that he had never met the Lord. He feared that, if identified with Christ, he would have to endure persecution for his faith.

Hear him speak now with freedom and power. Not only is he pointedly accusing the nation Israel of being responsible for the Lord's death, but is affirming that they will be held accountable for what they had done.

In his second sermon Peter said, "But you disowned the Holy and Righteous One, and asked for a murderer to be granted to you, but put to death the Prince of life, the One whom God raised from the dead, a fact to which we are witnesses" (Acts 3:14-15). These are not the words of a man who is afraid to die for his faith! He knew that he would be an open target for the political and ecclesiastical authorities. Yet he walked into this new role with absolute confidence and faith.

Our days of religious freedom in America may be numbered. Today everyone is free to *believe* whatever he or she wishes, but woe to the person who suggests that his belief should be passed on to others! Religion, we are told, is a private matter, and therefore many oppose the idea that we should be free to share our faith, much less try to "convert" others to a particular religion

We have been so intimidated by the Supreme Court and liberal groups who insist that we should be "politically correct" that some Christians have not been willing to stand for righteousness. We have become so frightened by recent developments that many churches seek the advice of attorneys when they are about to oppose abortion, homosexual rights, or pornography. We have been frightened and reduced to nebulous silence.

Where did Peter get his strength? When Christ promised the Spirit, He said, "And I will ask the Father, and He will give you another Helper, that He may be with you forever; that is the Spirit of truth, whom the world cannot receive, because it does not behold Him or know Him, but you know Him because He abides with you, and will be in you. I will not leave you as orphans; I will come to you" (John 14:16-18). In Greek there are two words for *another*. One means "similar" and the other means "the same." Christ uses the second word here, indicating that the Holy Spirit would be a helper who would be *the same as Christ Himself was on this earth*. In other words, the Holy Spirit has come to take the place of Christ's physical presence; that's why the Spirit could not be fully poured out until Christ had gone to heaven and been glorified.

Christ said, "It is to your advantage that I go away; for if I do not go away, the Helper shall not come to you" (16:7). When He was here on earth, Jesus could only be at one place at one time with His physical body. Now that He has gone to heaven and sent the Spirit, He is just as present with us as He was with the disciples on earth so long ago. The Helper, the Holy Spirit, stands where we stand; He sits where we sit; He listens when we talk; and endures what we see. He never leaves us nor forsakes us, and we can be assured of His presence no matter what.

When both fear and faith come to lodge in the harbor of

our hearts, it is important that only faith be allowed to cast anchor. And when we serve in faith, we know that we are not alone. The Spirit who energized timid Peter is the same One who gives us boldness to declare God's Word with confidence and power.

From Discouragement to Determination

When Christ was crucified, the disciples forsook Him and fled. Though they were rejuvenated when they learned of the Resurrection, they had many questions about what they would do after the Ascension. But let us notice the transformation that the Holy Spirit brought about and the determination they now had.

After the apostles were thrown into prison, we read that the authorities were influenced by Gamaliel. "And they took his advice; and after calling the apostles in, they flogged them and ordered them to speak no more in the name of Jesus, and then released them. So they went on their way from the presence of the Council, rejoicing that they had been considered worthy to suffer shame for His name. And every day, in the temple and from house to house, they kept right on teaching and preaching Jesus as the Christ" (Acts 5:40-42). The greater the whippings, the greater the witness!

The first change we've noticed affected Peter's *mind*—he now had spiritual understanding. The second moved his *emotions,* from fear to confidence and boldness. The third was a transformed *will:* Nothing could deter him from obeying the command of Christ. Here, despite being flogged—that is, whipped with thirty-nine lashes—the disciples rejoiced in the honor of bearing both pain and shame for Christ's name.

Notice in passing that being filled with the Spirit did not protect the apostles from physical violence. They were beaten, and later many of these apostles would be killed for their faith. The Holy Spirit did not exempt them from the flogging, but gave them grace to endure it. The Holy Spirit does not shield us from accidents, abuse, or the injustices common to man. He *does* supply the grace to endure these for the glory of Christ.

Think of the thousands of martyrs who died in Rome without protection from the flames or wild beasts. Yet, many testified that the Holy Spirit gave them the inner resources to cope with the outward pressures. Peter and the other apostles walked away from their beatings filled with joy; they felt honored that they had the privilege of suffering for Christ. Emotional wholeness and stability gave rise to a determination to serve God all the more faithfully. From house to house, and every day in the temple, they "kept right on teaching and preaching Jesus as the Christ."

It would be a big mistake to assume that such power was given to Peter simply because he was one of the apostles or because he was a spiritual leader in the church. The New Testament teaches that the same Spirit that indwelt Peter is ours as well. He indwells us so that we need not be a prisoner to our weaknesses, fears, and apprehensions. The transformation can reach down to the mind, emotion, and will. Yes, we too can be different.

Many Christians believe that the doctrine of the filling of the Holy Spirit is too mysterious, too far beyond the reach of the average Christian. They think that only missionaries and perhaps pastors are worthy to attain this spiritual blessing.

Not so. Christ invited people to come to Him to slake their spiritual thirst. Then we read, "But this He spoke of the Spirit, whom those who believed in Him were to receive; for the Spirit was not yet given, because Jesus was not yet glorified" (John 7:39). Please bear in mind that, just as we look to the cross for our forgiveness, so we must look to the ascended Christ for the gift of the Holy Spirit.

If you were to buy a book that came in two volumes, and

if you were to leave one of them at the counter, you could return and receive it without an additional charge. In the same way Christ gave us a two-volume gift; there is forgiveness and spiritual power. Both are ours when we believe in Christ. The forgiveness is based on the cross and the power is based on the Ascension. Both are our inheritance.

Yes, the Holy Spirit is a gift, but He is also a *compassionate* gift. In contrast to demons, who drive people compulsively, bringing despair and tyranny, the Holy Spirit is gentle and His ministry is often neglected. He is represented as a dove, a bird so sensitive that if insulted or ignored it folds its wings. Thankfully, the Spirit does not leave us when we disobey, but eventually, if we continue to disobey, we will no longer hear His voice. This explains why there are Christians who live in overt sin; they no longer hear the voice of the Spirit. God is quite unreal to them because their depression, guilt, and despair overrides the Spirit's ministry. That's why Paul said, "And do not grieve the Holy Spirit of God, by whom you were sealed for the day of redemption" (Eph. 4:30).

When we walk with the Spirit in sensitivity, He will enable us to hold our tongue; we will be prevented from sinning; we will be able to turn away from evil; and we will be ridded of the addictions that might plague us. And we will have the courage to share our faith, even if people consider us part of the "lunatic fringe."

The power of the Spirit increases as self-will decreases. We do not need psychological mechanisms to cope with the pressures of life. We need more faith, more surrender, more of the cross. Our Lord said, "Truly, truly, I say to you, unless a grain of wheat falls into the earth and dies, it remains by itself alone; but if it dies, it bears much fruit" (John 12:24). This death to self means coming to the end of our own self-determination.

Wheat buried in pyramids for 4,000 years grew when

planted. Though the life was dormant throughout these many centuries, the right conditions caused the kernel to spring up with new life. Just so the sunshine of God's love and the soil of His Word can give us life, if we are willing to die to our own plans and ambitions. Yieldedness can be half-hearted and conditional; it can also be complete and final. Only such submission brings the full blessing of the Spirit.

The Spirit does not push us but leads us; He does not prod us with compulsion but with tenderness. But only those who have died to self-will can enjoy the gift of His presence. Peter was all too ordinary, but he depended upon the Spirit with extraordinary faith. It's not what we have that is important, it is whether it has been placed in Christ's hands that makes the difference. The Spirit is *resident* but only we can make Him *president*.

The chisel of circumstances combines with the sovereignty of the Spirit to make us live for Christ. Mind, emotion, and will obey the divine initiative. The work the Sculptor begins He delights to finish.

Peter felt that touch and so can we.

Chapter Eleven

THE TRACE
OF HIS SHADOW

(Read Acts 3:1-10; 5:1-11; 8:14-24; 10:44-48)

Very likely you remember those people who have had a special impact in your life. Just at the right time you may have been given advice by a schoolteacher, or possibly a Christian friend supported you during a particularly difficult time of suffering. In my case, it was praying parents that God used to keep my life on track.

By the influence of a loving touch, the encouragement of friends, or the sharing of the Gospel—in all these ways we leave our imprint in the sands of life. Such influences are recorded and Christ assured us that even a cup of cold water given in His name would not go unnoticed.

When the Holy Spirit came on the Day of Pentecost, a small band of men and women had a profound effect on their generation, and yes, they impact us even today. We are encouraged by how they stood for Christ at great personal cost. God gave them the ability to speak in languages they had never learned, and healings took place to confirm their power and authority. Peter had such a gift of doing miracles that "they even carried the sick out into the streets, and laid them on cots and pallets, so that when Peter came by, at least his shadow might fall on any one of them" (Acts 5:15). Though not explicitly stated, it is reasonable to assume that when Peter's shadow fell on individuals they were actually healed. God was with Peter in a powerful, demonstrable way.

All of us cast a shadow, whether for good or for ill, as we walk through the corridors of life. We all leave our world a little better or a little worse. Nothing we touch remains the same.

Let's look at three snapshots in Peter's life in which his "shadow," his influence, affected the lives of others.

The Shadow of a Healing Touch

In Acts 3 we read that a man who had been lame from his mother's womb was set down every day at the gate of the temple to beg as worshipers walked by. Though this man was beside the gate of the magnificent temple area, he was in a pitiful state. Some friends had laid him there so that he could beg. And, as far as he was concerned, he was condemned to a life of continued misery.

As Peter and John walked by, the cripple looked up hoping to receive alms. But Peter saw beyond this physical need and with the eye of faith saw that Christ, the Prince of life, was near him. Here on the street was weakness, but in the Lord there was the power of life. In the presence of despair, there was hope.

This handicapped beggar was a picture of the nation Israel itself. Crippled, burdened with sin and helplessness, Israel had just rejected the Prince of life. The nation had resisted the One who could heal its innermost soul. If only the people would have accepted Christ's healing touch.

Peter, looking down at the man's helplessness, felt compassion. He had no money, but he had something far better. More important than silver and gold was the restoration of robust strength to this discouraged man!

Then Peter said, "I do not possess silver and gold, but what I do have I give to you: In the name of Jesus Christ the

Nazarene—walk!" (3:6) Then Peter seized him by the right hand and raised him up, and immediately he stood upright and began to walk! The power of the resurrected Christ had connected with the withering form of a cripple. "And with a leap, he stood upright and began to walk; and he entered the temple with them, walking and leaping and praising God" (v. 8). Needless to say, this caused a sensation in the temple area, and those whose hearts were open to the Lord rejoiced.

F.B. Meyer says that there are four different kinds of people in the world: (1) There are those who have nothing to give—they have no silver or gold, no blessing, no encouragement, no helpfulness. They go through life without helping anyone, but simply withdraw into their own small world. Then, (2) there are those who have silver and gold but are not mighty in spirit—these people generally keep the silver and gold to themselves and do not give it. These are the paupers of the universe. Then, (3) there are those who, like Peter, have no silver or gold but are filled with faith, vision, encouragement, and a healing touch. These are rich unto God. Finally, (4) there are those who give silver and gold and spiritual riches besides. These also are rich toward God (*Peter,* p. 148).

Thomas Aquinas, it is said, went to visit the pope in Rome. When they saw the treasures of the Vatican, the pontiff remarked, "We cannot say as did the first pope, 'Silver and gold have I none.' " To which Aquinas replied, "Neither can you say, 'In the name of Jesus, rise up and walk!' "

Wealth is not the standard of value. The poverty of Christ is a powerful reminder that one does not have to be rich in this world's goods in order to be rich toward God. Christ taught that it was hard, if not impossible, for the rich to enter into the kingdom of heaven.

Christ does not expect us to give what we do not have. Most of us do not have the gift of healing, but we do have something equally precious, and even more important. We can give the gift of prayer, the gift of a listening ear, the gift of hospitality, the gift of compassion. And more important, we can offer to others the gift of eternal life.

More significant than this man's physical health was the fact that he almost certainly came to faith in Christ. The infusion of physical life was only a drop in the ocean in comparison to the eternal life he received through faith. He joyfully entered into the temple area, from which his congenital deformity had always excluded him. And when the people who knew him saw what had happened, God was glorified.

And what did Peter himself make of this startling event? He consciously deflected any praise by reminding the people that this miracle came not because of his own piety but because of the power of Christ. "And on the basis of faith in His name, it is the name of Jesus which has strengthened this man whom you see and know; and the faith which comes through Him has given him this perfect health in the presence of you all" (3:16).

As I look at my life, I see that I am the product of many other people's gifts. My parents who nurtured me and prayed for me, my friends who believed in me, and those people who gave me the opportunity to serve. Throughout my life I have been the happy recipient of the faithful influences of hundreds of people. Freely I have received, now it is my responsibility to freely give!

Peter's shadow transformed that paralyzed man. Our shadow can help men and women come to the Savior, who can bring them into an eternal abode. And as one person said, "If I can handle eternity, I should be able to handle today!"

The Shadow of a Stinging Rebuke

When the Holy Spirit came upon the Christian community, there was a spontaneous outpouring of generosity. "For there was not a needy person among them, for all who were owners of land or houses would sell them and bring the proceeds of the sales, and lay them at the apostles' feet; and they would be distributed to each, as any had need" (4:34-35).

This money was used for the apostles' living expenses; also, the widows and physically destitute would be given money according to their need. Participation was entirely voluntary; there was no stipulated amount to give. Some, like Barnabas, made great sacrifices simply because they felt privileged to have a part in the growing revival movement. Understandably, those who sold their possessions and gave the money to the apostles were held in high esteem. Those who wanted to keep their property were free to do so.

Ananias and his wife Sapphira wanted to share in the gratitude that came to the generous. They had heard how the people talked about the devotion of the likes of Barnabas, and thought they would also like to be held in high regard. They also, however, wanted to keep some of the money for themselves. So they sold a piece of property and "kept back some of the price." This was their right, of course.

What made their actions evil was not that they kept some of the money, but that they left the distinct *impression* that they were giving all of their money to the apostles. Let's say they sold their land for $1,000, but gave only $500 to the apostles. They gave the impression that the amount bequeathed to the leaders of the church was the total sale price of their land. It was, in effect, a "white lie."

But God knew the whole truth and communicated this to Peter, who said, "Ananias, why has Satan filled your heart to lie to the Holy Spirit, and to keep back some of the price of the land? While it remained unsold, did it not remain your own? And after it was sold, was it not under your control? Why is it that you have conceived this deed in your heart?

You have not lied to men, but to God" (5:3-4). Ananias then died at the hand of God, and moments later when his wife came through the door, she also died.

This penalty was severe, but God was impressing upon the hearts of the early church that, (1) all lies are directed against Him, and only in a secondary sense against people. After all, the Lord is the supreme lawgiver in the universe and it is *His laws* that are violated when we are untruthful. And, (2) we should not trifle with the truth when serving God (or any other time, for that matter). The reaction of the church to this immediate judgment was quite proper: "And great fear came upon the whole church, and upon all who heard these things" (v. 11).

Finally, (3) Satan was revealed to be a liar, and the author of lies. He injected these thoughts into this couple's minds without their being aware of it. They thought that this deception was just their own idea, and that's why they were not frightened by the decision to be dishonest. But God took their hypocrisy seriously and used them as a powerful lesson for us all.

Yes, sometimes Peter's shadow was a healing touch, but it could also be a stinging rebuke. Not all of our influence needs to be encouraging in order for it to be effective. Sometimes we must point out sin and be hated for it. Our goal, of course, is the restoration of God's children to fellowship with the Almighty and fellowship with others. Not everyone will respond, yet such difficult assignments are also part of our responsibility and influence.

The Shadow of the Gospel's Outreach

In Acts 8 Philip went to Samaria to preach the Gospel and multitudes believed. But God withheld the gift of the Holy Spirit until Peter and John went to the Samaritans and laid hands on them. "Then they began laying their hands on them, and they were receiving the Holy Spirit" (8:17). To-day, whenever a person receives Christ as Savior, he or she immediately receives the gift of the Holy Spirit. But the Book of Acts is the story of the transition of the church from infancy to adulthood. Because of the strong rivalry between the Jews and the Samaritans, it was very important that the apostles come to Samaria to prove the unity of the church.

Peter and John's presence gave the assurance that the same Holy Spirit who came to the church in Jerusalem had now come to those who were considered outcasts (the Samaritans). And so Peter became one of the leaders in opening the door of the Gospel to this despised ethnic group. He was beginning to exercise the "keys of the kingdom."

There was another door that Peter would soon open. The next circle of people to be welcomed into the church were the Gentiles (Acts 10). Cornelius, who lived in Caesarea, was an unusual man. He was an earnest seeker after God, having become weary of the paganism widely practiced in that day. When he came in contact with the Old Testament, even though he was a Gentile he became convinced that it was a revelation from God. His soul became so hungry for God that he began to pray continuously and do good deeds in an attempt to become a proselyte, a convert to Judaism. Yet, for all this, he did not yet know that he needed to put his faith in Israel's Messiah, the Lord Jesus Christ.

God was not unmindful of this man's search for spiritual reality. The angel that came to him said, "Your prayers and your alms have ascended as a memorial before God" (10:4). At exactly 3 o'clock one afternoon Cornelius had a vision. An angel of God came to tell him to send a delegation to Joppa to find Peter, who was residing in a house beside the sea thirty miles away. His men left immediately, but understandably did not make the entire thirty-mile journey that afternoon.

The next day at 12 noon, God gave Peter a special vision that would free him from his legalistic roots, so he would know that God had also opened the door to the Gentiles. Peter was resting on the housetop waiting for lunch. Though he was hungry he fell asleep and in a trance saw the sky open, and an object like a great sheet came down, lowered by four corners to the ground. On it were all kinds of four-footed animals that Jews were forbidden to eat according to Old Testament law. A voice came to him, "Arise, Peter, kill and eat!" (10:13) But he refused, insisting that these animals were "unclean." But the voice persisted, "What God has cleansed, no longer consider unholy" (v. 15).

As Peter was reflecting on this vision, the men Cornelius had sent came looking for him. He listened to their incredible story about the desire of Cornelius to know more about the true God; then they related the vision this Gentile had received. The timing was perfect!

Now Peter understood the full meaning of his own vision: God was trying to tell him that the distinctions between Jews and Gentiles detailed in the Old Testament were gone. He could actually enter the home of a Gentile and share the good news of the Gospel. This was a radical departure from what he had been taught.

The next day Peter started on the journey, and the following day arrived at the home of Cornelius. After becoming acquainted he made this announcement: "I most certainly understand now that God is not one to show partiality, but in every nation the man who fears Him and does what is right, is welcome to Him" (vv. 34-35). Then followed a presentation of the Gospel. While Peter was still speaking, the Holy Spirit fell on those who were listening to his message. And as further proof that the Gentiles were now included in God's program, the new believers spoke in tongues and were baptized in water. Once again Peter was exercising his right to open the doors of the Gospel. The "keys" had opened another door.

It is worth noting that God used an angel to communicate with Cornelius. This angel did not reveal the Gospel, but rather told Cornelius how to get in contact with a man who could bring him the Good News. The angels of heaven could have delivered sermons more effectively than Peter. But God's plan is to use men and women, no matter how imperfect they may be. His chisel was applied to Peter, not to the angels that surrounded Him.

One result of Peter's visit to Cornelius was that he was criticized for eating in the home of a Gentile. This, according to Old Testament law, was not just a breach of etiquette but also a doctrinal compromise. But Peter defended his actions by telling the other apostles the whole story. When his explanation was finished, we read, "And when they heard this, they quieted down, and glorified God, saying, 'Well then, God has granted to the Gentiles also the repentance that leads to life' " (11:18).

And so as Peter moved through life, his shadow affected everyone he met. Whether it was a healing touch, a stinging rebuke, or a joyful opportunity, no one was the same after they had been in the presence of this remarkable man.

Your Shadow and Mine

What about our shadow? Let's remember that the greatest impact we can have is not the silver and gold we can give but the life we can live. The shadow of a person in his home, in his business, or out on the street—that shadow has effects that will continue throughout all eternity. When you throw a stone in a pond, the ripples continue even after the stone has sunk to the bottom. Long after we are gone, either for good or for ill, our influence will continue.

Also, our greatest impact is frequently unconscious. We

influence others by the way we live, not just by what we say. When people are watching, we tend to be on our best behavior. But when we are positive role models even when we think no one is watching—that kind of an impact is long-lasting and special to God.

Finally, our shadow is dependent on our relationship to the Son. Only those who live in the light will cast a shadow that is positive, effective, and eternal. When we walk in darkness, there is no shadow—no influence that will make those around us better people. Some people live only for themselves, and they will die as they have lived. Someone has said, "In eternity we become what we are now only more so." The selfish and the wicked will become even more selfish and wicked after death. The righteous will become more generous, more loving, and more joyful.

Perhaps you and I are discouraged today and feel as if we have nothing to give. But let me remind you that once we have received the gift of the Spirit, we can all give to someone else. God doesn't expect us to give what we do not have, but He gives to us that we might give back in return. "Freely you have received, freely give."

A.J. Gordon tells of seeing a man in the distance pumping water, and wondering how a human being could work so consistently and tirelessly. But as he came nearer, he realized that it was not a man that was doing the pumping, but rather a figure of a man, which was itself being pumped by an artesian well as the water gushed through the pipe system. Just so, it is not that we must give what we do not have; rather, because Christ promised the Holy Spirit who would create rivers of living waters within us, we all have something to give today.

Wherever our shadow is cast, we will affect the lives of others and receive a lasting reward. But only those who look at the Son will have a shadow that continues forever.

Chapter Twelve

KEPT IN
THE MASTER'S HAND

(Read Acts 12:1-25)

God expects us to see His hand even in the night of our experience. Often we must descend into darkness in order to see the light. To those who have faith, God's fingerprint can often be spotted in the most unlikely places.

We've learned that God transformed Peter from an impulsive, fearful man to a leader with strength and even-tempered dependability. As the one who was given "the keys of the kingdom," he proclaimed the Gospel to the Samaritans and the Gentiles undeterred by formidable obstacles. Under the good hand of God he also performed remarkable miracles, and had the privilege of looking back on a life filled with the clear evidence of God's guidance.

But there were times when it appeared as if Peter's enemies would triumph. By all appearances, his life was on the verge of being cut short. God put Peter in a corner with no known way of escape. His future was to be determined by forces beyond his control. Like a driver whose steering wheel becomes disconnected, there are times when our fate is quite literally out of our hands.

Yet these experiences only deepened Peter's walk of faith. His knowledge of God and His ways blossomed in the midst of a fiery trial that might have intimidated a lesser man.

Though it was dark on earth, Peter knew that the lights were on in heaven.

Recall that on the night Christ was betrayed, Peter had promised, "Lord, with You I am ready to go both to prison and to death" (Luke 22:33). But that very night he slept when he should have been praying, and later that same evening denied his Lord.

Now fourteen years have passed. On several occasions Peter had fulfilled the first part of his promise; he spent many nights in jail because of his love for Christ. In Acts 12 we have the dramatic story of one of those imprisonments and a miraculous escape. The story weaves together three links in the chain of divine providence that testify to the sovereign power and wisdom of God.

Peter Was Arrested

We read, "Now about that time Herod the king laid hands on some who belonged to the church, in order to mistreat them" (Acts 12:1). This is a reference to Herod Agrippa I, the grandson of Herod the Great who had the male infants killed when Christ was born in Bethlehem. This grandson, who was known for his cruelty, delighted in pleasing the Jews. As a trial balloon, he killed James, the brother of John, with the sword. "And when he saw that it pleased the Jews, he proceeded to arrest Peter also. Now it was during the days of the Feast of Unleavened Bread. And when he had seized him, he put him in prison, delivering him to four squads of soldiers to guard him, intending after the Passover to bring him out before the people. So Peter was kept in the prison, but prayer for him was being made fervently by the church to God" (12:3-5).

Peter was arrested unjustly, for he had violated neither moral nor political laws. His only crime was to displease the arbitrary whim of the king. Cruel fate appeared to work against Peter and now he was scheduled to die by the sword.

Today when we put ourselves in a similar situation, we immediately think of the legal recourse that we would have in a just court of law. But of course in biblical times tyrants ruled by their caprice, not by just laws. Peter had no opportunity to have a hearing to clear his name. In 1988, John Demjanjuk of Cleveland, Ohio was condemned to die by an Israeli court because they believed he was "Ivan the Terrible," the cruel director of one of Hitler's death camps. But thankfully, he has been able to appeal to both American and Israeli law in the effort to prove his innocence. Peter had to entrust his case solely to God without a hint of human help in sight.

But God followed Peter into prison. Our Lord does not have to restrict His entry to the posted visiting hours. He does not observe the restrictions we do when we take a friend to the airport and come to the sign, "Passengers Only beyond This Point." As Joseph learned, God goes with His people into the dungeon, and accompanies them when they cross a border from one country to another. He goes with us to the school, the factory, the home, and the hospital. "For He Himself has said, 'I will never desert you, nor will I ever forsake you,' so that we may confidently say, 'The Lord is my helper, I will not be afraid. What shall man do to me?' " (Heb. 13:5-6)

Peter found himself in a dungeon with sixteen soldiers assigned to guard him. Probably they worked in shifts of four—one was chained to each of Peter's arms, one guarded the entrance of the dungeon, and the other guarded the entrance to the prison itself. Thus sixteen soldiers on six-hour shifts worked round the clock to make sure that Peter would stay put. After all, he had had a history of jailbreaks! Herod may have heard of his miraculous deliverance years before. The king's reputation was at stake, so no one took any chances.

What were the odds of Peter escaping alive? Not great. The only light in the darkness is found in one short phrase, "But prayer for him was being made fervently by the church to God" (Acts 12:5). Clarence McCartney writes, "Never were there greater odds against prayer. On one side, Herod, the sixteen soldiers, the grim fortress walls of the dungeon, and the power of Rome itself; on the other side, a handful of men and women in a prayer meeting. How unequal the combat! And yet, as has often happened since, it was the prayer meeting that came out victorious" (*Peter and His Lord*, p. 211).

Peter was in prison according to the plan and purposes of God. Divine Providence had led him to the dungeon. Only Divine Providence could plan that he would get out alive. On the very night before Herod was planning to bring Peter out of prison to execute him, Peter was asleep between two soldiers. His sleep in the Garden of Gethsemane fourteen years earlier was the sleep of carelessness; the sleep here in the dungeon was the *sleep of faith*. God "gives His beloved sleep" (Ps. 127:2, KJV) when they entrust their lives wholly to His care. Peter knew his fate was not in Herod's hands.

Peter Was Rescued

There is a second link in the chain of Divine Providence. We read:

> And behold, an angel of the Lord suddenly appeared, and a light shone in the cell; and he struck Peter's side and roused him, saying, "Get up quickly." And his chains fell off his hands. And the angel said to him, "Gird yourself and put on your sandals." And he did so. And he said to him, "Wrap your cloak around you and follow me." And he went out and continued to follow, and he did not know that what was being done by the

angel was real, but thought he was seeing a vision. And when they had passed the first and second guard, they came to the iron gate that leads into the city, which opened for them by itself; and they went out and went along one street; and immediately the angel departed from him (Acts 12:7-10).

Here was a judicious use of divine power. The Lord had *power over people,* for the guards had to sleep through this ordeal. Apparently they were given some cosmic sleeping pills so that they would be unaware of the miracle happening before their weary eyes. They saw no light; they heard no feet. Not even the watchful eye of soldiers can thwart the purposes of God.

Then, also, the Lord had *power over matter,* for the chains fell off and the iron gate opened up just as it does for us when we leave a supermarket! No obstacle—whether the human will of a soldier or inanimate nature—can stand in the way of the purposes of God.

The rest of the story is well-known: Peter walked out into the cool night air and realized that he had not been dreaming. He immediately went to the house of Mary the mother of John Mark, where the church was praying. "And when he knocked at the door of the gate, a servant girl named Rhoda came to answer. And when she recognized Peter's voice, because of her joy she did not open the gate, but ran in and announced that Peter was standing in front of the gate" (vv. 13-14).

We might expect that these dear saints would believe her! They were praying in the will of God, with a measure of faith that Peter would be miraculously delivered from the death that awaited him. But they had two alternate explanations for Rhoda's excited remarks. (1) They said, "You are mad!" This servant girl, they feared, had buckled under the emotional stress that persecution was causing. And should that explanation be inadequate, they had another: (2) "It is his angel"! (v. 15)

Amazing, isn't it, that some of God's seasoned saints have an explanation for everything! Sometimes it is so difficult for us to believe that God answers prayer that when He does, we attribute His goodness to natural causes. Ironically, *Peter was able to get out of the gate of the prison but he was not able to get through the gate into the prayer meeting!*

God waited until the faith of His people had almost expired and then did a miracle at the very moment it was needed. Peter was not missed until the morning, so he must have escaped sometime between 3 A.M., when a fresh foursome of soldiers had come on duty, and 6 A.M., when they would have been relieved. In a classic understatement, Luke reports, "Now when day came, there was no small disturbance among the soldiers as to what could have become of Peter" (v. 18). In anger Herod had these guards executed.

Peter Was Vindicated

A third link in God's providential chain was the death of Herod. This king went to Caesarea and, according to Josephus, dressed in shimmering silver to deliver an address to his followers. We read, "And the people kept crying out, 'The voice of a god and not of a man!' And immediately an angel of the Lord struck him because he did not give God the glory, and he was eaten by worms and died" (vv. 22-23).

Josephus, in his *Antiquities of the Jews,* gives us the details of this event. He describes the great multitude that came to see Herod, who on the second day put on the garment of silver tissue. Some of his followers cried out that he was a god and not a man. Then a severe pain arose within him and he showed signs of violent torment. Five days later he died.

Obviously, the king should not have received the worship

that was coming in his direction. When the people wanted to deify him, he should have pointed out that he was indeed only a man. But because he took the glory that belongs to God alone, he was smitten and died a painful death of worms.

An important phrase in this chapter is repeated. In verse 7 we read that an angel of the Lord struck Peter, and in verse 23 we read that an angel of the Lord struck Herod. Of course I can't prove it, but I believe that this was the same angel! The angel struck Peter to awaken him to the fact that something good was about to happen in his life. But the angel struck Herod to let him know that something bad was about to come upon him. At one time the angel was a messenger of life and hope; at the other time he was a messenger of death and despair.

But what does all this mean? Why these providential links in God's plan for Peter's life? The Lord never performs miracles simply that we might stand in awe of His power. He does not open an iron gate to fascinate the curious and to close the mouths of the unbelieving world. There is always a hidden purpose, insights that we must learn from these providential occurrences.

Here are three lessons that Peter learned as a result of the miracle God did in Jerusalem:

First, *God is sovereign*. Notice that James was killed with the sword but Peter lived. The martyr was James, the son of Zebedee, the brother of the Apostle John. He was among the three most favored disciples, present at the Mount of Transfiguration and invited by Christ to share the agony of Gethsemane. Did God abandon James? Though we do not even know what this martyr's final words were, we can be confident that he too was a man of faith. And the Lord was with him to the end, though his life was cut short. He too died within the will of God.

Of course the church was praying for Peter's release, but perhaps they had prayed for James as well. Regardless, God could have delivered James with or without the people's prayers, and He could have done the same for Peter quite apart from prayer. We know that the church was praying within God's will though not with an overabundance of faith. But the fact is that God wanted James to *die* for His glory, and He wanted Peter to *live* for His glory. And only God makes those choices.

Have you ever wondered how Peter was able to sleep, even though he knew that he had been scheduled to be executed in the morning? It may well be that he had the assurance in his heart that he would not die as a victim of Herod's sword. Fourteen years before, Christ had personally given him a promise: " 'Truly, truly, I say to you, when you were younger, you used to gird yourself, and walk wherever you wished; but when you grow old, you will stretch out your hands, and someone else will gird you, and bring you where you do not wish to go.' Now this He said, signifying by what kind of death he would glorify God" (John 21:18-19).

Peter knew, (1) that he would grow to be an old man, and, (2) that his death would occur by the stretching out of his arms. Tradition says that Peter died a martyr, crucified upside down because he did not think himself worthy to be crucified in the same position as the Master whom he so fervently loved. With these words lodged in his heart, Peter was able to sleep in prison knowing that his hour had not yet come.

Peter slept because he trusted in the promise of Jesus. He knew that no combination of demons and men would kill him until his work was done. Of course we envy Peter, wishing that we ourselves had a specific word from the lips of Christ, just for us. But we do have such a word: "Peace I leave with you; My peace I give to you; not as the world gives, do I give to you. Let not your heart be troubled, nor let it be fearful" (14:27). Yes, God is sovereign and we can rest on His promises, knowing that our fate is in His hands.

Second, Peter had to learn that *God is triumphant.* This chapter opens with Herod in control, having killed James and with specific plans to kill Peter. Interestingly, it closes with Peter alive and well and Herod dying a shameful, excruciating death. We should never judge the circumstances of life by their appearance, but in light of God's eternal plan. This chapter is a microcosm of the reversal of fortune that Satan and his powers will have in the final day. The devil always loses, even when it appears he is winning. Only the final battle really matters.

"The wicked plots against the righteous, and gnashes at him with his teeth. The Lord laughs at him; for He sees his day is coming" (Ps. 37:12-13).

Finally, Peter had to learn that *God is powerful.* God can open an iron gate and cause alert soldiers to fall asleep. He can do as He wishes with the forces of nature and the evil intentions of men. *Even when we are in the hands of men, we are actually in the hands of God.*

How much better to be in prison bound with chains, yet free in spirit, than to be in a palace, bound by the ravages of condemnation or self-serving anger that torments the soul! There are dungeons far worse than the barren prisons of Jerusalem or Rome. Herod, though technically free, was enslaved by powers stronger than the soldiers he had charged to keep Peter bound.

Perhaps you feel imprisoned within your home, job, school, or factory. You may feel chained to circumstances or subject to the whims of those about you. Worse, you may feel the inner torment of shame, frustration, and anger that others have caused. There may not be an easy way out of your private torture chamber, and I suggest you seek the help of a trusted and wise friend. But I also urge you to remember God's promises, and to accept the peace that He has promised.

You may be in a prison of your own making. I'm reminded of a blacksmith during the Middle Ages who bragged that no one could ever break the chains he made. Then one day he was imprisoned, and looked at the chains that bound him and found his own mark. There is a prison of the soul, the prison of fear, of guilt, of regret—these and a thousand other voices cry out for freedom.

When Christ was in Nazareth, He went into the synagogue and read from Isaiah the prophet: "The Spirit of the Lord is upon Me, because He anointed Me to preach the Gospel to the poor. He has sent Me to proclaim release to the captives, and recovery of sight to the blind, to set free those who are downtrodden, to proclaim the favorable year of the Lord" (Luke 4:18-19). Our Lord is a specialist at freeing prisoners!

Peter's prison experience reminds us that there is no chain that is too strong, there is no dungeon that is too deep, there is no gate that is too high but that God is greater still.

Charles Wesley, the brother of John Wesley the famous revivalist, often meditated on his own spiritual conversion. After months of agony, questioning, and doubt, the light of the Gospel dawned upon his soul and he felt as if he had been loosed from a fearful personal prison. To celebrate this great liberation, he wrote the song, "And Can It Be That I Should Gain?" one of the greatest hymns of all time. Notice the powerful imagery of this spiritual prisoner experiencing the freedom of Christ:

> Long my imprisoned spirit lay
> Fast bound in sin and nature's night;
> Thine eye diffused a quick'ning ray,

I woke, the dungeon flamed with light;
My chains fell off, my heart was free;
I rose, went forth, and followed Thee.
Amazing love! How can it be
That Thou, my God, shouldst die for me.

Peter's body was in prison, but his heart was free. Even in darkness there was morning in his heart. The fearful Peter had been changed into the fearless Peter. The sand had become a rock.

As always, Christ's promise had come to pass.

Epilogue
THE LEGACY OF ONE LIFE

If we want to leave God's fingerprints on what we do on earth, it only stands to reason that we must put our life in His hands! *Only He can take what we do and make it last forever.*

God has put eternity in every man's heart. Intuitively we seek both for meaning and value, hoping to leave a legacy that will continue long after we have departed this earth. Apart from our relationship with God, no such impact is even remotely possible. Only a Creator can confer dignity upon us, and only by His grace can we hope to make a contribution that lasts.

Peter the fisherman had an influence that continues until this day, and only heaven will reveal the full impact of his faithfulness. Because Peter stood as he did with Christ at the beginning of the church, we have all been positively affected by his life, witness, and writings. The Christ who used the chisel to sculpt Peter, now uses Peter to sculpt us. We also are now being fashioned by the Divine Hand.

Let us never forget that we, like Peter, can also make a lasting contribution to the service of Christ. True, not one of us will ever write a book that will be a part of the inspired Scripture; probably not one of us will live a life that will be the subject of sermons and books; not one of us will influence untold millions through our knowledge of Christ and our example in martyrdom. But God does not expect us to do what Peter did. He only expects us to serve with the same love, single-mindedness, and faith. The consistent teaching of

Christ is that those who have few talents can receive the same reward as those with many. Indeed, a cup of cold water given in Christ's name will not go unnoticed.

We can join Peter if we follow his lead in obedience and love. We can, in our own way, do what he did and receive the same reward. His influence, like ours, will go on forever because of:

What We Believe

Let us join Peter in his confession that Christ is "the Son of the Living God." If we do, the same miracle God wrought in Peter's heart has taken place in ours. And with our faith we become members of the church that Christ promised to build.

Peter had the privilege of being on the Mount of Transfiguration where he heard the voice of the Father say, "This is My beloved Son with whom I am well pleased" (2 Peter 1:17). How we might wish that we could have joined that small company! Yet, Peter himself taught that, though we were not with Christ on earth, we have not missed anything that would hinder our walk with Him. His experience on the Mount of Transfiguration, he says, only makes the prophetic word "more sure, to which you do well to pay attention as to a lamp shining in a dark place, until the day dawns and the morning star arises in your hearts" (v. 19). Through the Word we can have an experience that is just as certain as his!

North of British Columbia, the Fraser River rushes down a mountainside, then separates into two powerful streams, one going to the Atlantic and the other to the Pacific Ocean. This point in the river is known as the Great Divide. Christ also is a *Great Divide,* a Man who separates humanity into two separate groups—heaven and hell; eternal life and eternal misery.

Our faith is just as firmly rooted as Peter's was in Christ's deity and in His death for us. In believing what Peter believed, we share his reward.

What We Do

What did Peter do with what he knew? He shared his faith with all who would listen. Whether on the Day of Pentecost or in the house of Cornelius, he explained the truths of the Gospel. He never tired of telling others that Christ's death at the hands of evil men was God's providential response to man's need. Sin nailed Him there, but through faith He became the Sin-bearer for those who believe.

Peter also was able to do miracles to confirm the wonderful works of God. Although this gift seems to have faded after the times of the apostles, we also have the opportunity to do good works. As Christ promised, no one who leaves father or mother will be unrewarded for his commitment. And those who are faithful in the least will be granted a greater place in the kingdom.

Remember that God never lets us see the full impact our good deeds have here on earth. All this is hidden from us, though it will be revealed at the Judgment Seat of Christ. Every good deed sets in motion a series of "domino effects" that stretch to eternity. We have no idea of the hidden connections that fit into the divine mosaic.

Perhaps the reason the dead are not rewarded immediately for their good deeds, but must wait until the Rapture, is so that the effects of their lives may be fully seen. " 'Blessed are the dead who die in the Lord from now on!' 'Yes,' says the Spirit, 'That they may rest from their labors, for their deeds follow with them' " (Rev. 14:13).

What We Become

"Character," said D.L. Moody, "is what a man is in the dark." What we do *for* God is not as important as what God does *in us.* This is why Peter listed the virtues for which we must strive, with God's help. Here ultimately is the secret of true greatness.

> For by these He has granted to us His precious and magnificent promises, in order that by them you might become partakers of the divine nature, having escaped the corruption that is in the world by lust. Now for this very reason also, applying all diligence, in your faith supply moral excellence, and in your moral excellence, knowledge; and in your knowledge, self-control, and in your self-control, perseverance, and in your perseverance, godliness; and in your godliness, brotherly kindness, and in your brotherly kindness, Christian love. For if these qualities are yours and are increasing, they render you neither useless nor unfruitful in the true knowledge of our Lord Jesus Christ (2 Peter 1:4-8).

Why should we give ourselves single-mindedly to such character qualities? Because when Christ returns and the earth is burned up, all that will last are the people we have influenced and the inner lives we have developed. Cars, clothes, status, and pleasure—all these end at the beginning of eternity. Only faith, hope, and love, along with the fruit of godly character, will pass from this life to the next.

From Peter we learn:

1. *Everyone has an eternal impact.*

Yes, even unbelievers will live eternally, in the presence of their own sin and rebellion. Believers will live eternally in heaven, rewarded for the degree of their faithfulness while on earth. The purpose of life is preparation for eternity.

2. *Our lives are a mixture of good deeds and bad; wheat and chaff.*

Even after about fourteen years of courageous, powerful

ministry, Peter still returned to his past fears. None other than the Apostle Paul himself had to rebuke Peter when his actions were contrary to the Gospel. To quote Paul, "But when Cephas came to Antioch, I opposed him to his face, because he stood condemned" (Gal. 2:11). Then follows an explanation: Specifically, Peter was influenced by the Judaizers (who insisted that it was necessary to become a Jew to be saved). Out of fear Peter stopped eating with Gentiles and appeared to be agreeing with the Jewish legalists. Paul publicly rebuked him for his inconsistency.

Peter had his failures, his moments of doubt and fear. He was far from perfect, but he strove to develop the positive and diminish the negative. As someone has said, it is not where you are spiritually that is as important as the direction you are moving. It is not what we do but for whom we do it that makes the difference.

3. *Ultimately, only God's evaluation, and not man's opinion, really matters.*

Who cares about the plans of the Sanhedrin, or the intentions of a Herod? It has always been God's plan to win with few rather than with many. It has also been His plan to wait until eternity to reveal the full extent of His undiminished victory.

Tradition says Peter died a martyr (perhaps in Rome) and requested that he be crucified upside down, for he felt unworthy to die in the same posture as his Master. Like the ancient lamplighter, future generations can see the legacy that he left and the light he left behind.

And we have the opportunity to share in his reward.